Scaling the Tail

Other Palgrave Pivot titles

Liz Montegary and Melissa Autumn White (editors): **Mobile Desires: The Politics and Erotics of Mobility Justice**

Anna Larsson and Sanja Magdalenić: **Sociology in Sweden: A History**

Philip Whitehead: **Reconceptualising the Moral Economy of Criminal Justice: A New Perspective**

Thomas Kaiserfeld: **Beyond Innovation: Technology, Institution and Change as Categories for Social Analysis**

Dirk Jacob Wolfson: **The Political Economy of Sustainable Development: Valuation, Distribution, Governance**

Twyla J. Hill: **Family Caregiving in Aging Populations**

Alexander M. Stoner and Andony Melathopoulos: **Freedom in the Anthropocene: Twentieth Century Helplessness in the Face of Climate Change**

Christine J. Hong: **Identity, Youth, and Gender in the Korean American Christian Church**

Cenap Çakmak and Murat Ustaoğlu: **Post-Conflict Syrian State and Nation Building: Economic and Political Development**

Richard J. Arend: **Wicked Entrepreneurship: Defining the Basics of Entreponerology**

Rubén Arcos and Randolph H. Pherson (editors): **Intelligence Communication in the Digital Era: Transforming Security, Defence and Business**

Jane L. Chapman, Dan Ellin and Adam Sherif: **Comics, the Holocaust and Hiroshima**

AKM Ahsan Ullah, Mallik Akram Hossain and Kazi Maruful Islam: **Migration and Worker Fatalities Abroad**

Debra Reddin van Tuyll, Nancy McKenzie Dupont and Joseph R. Hayden: **Journalism in the Fallen Confederacy**

Michael Gardiner: **Time, Action and the Scottish Independence Referendum**

Tom Bristow: **The Anthropocene Lyric: An Affective Geography of Poetry, Person, Place**

Shepard Masocha: **Asylum Seekers, Social Work and Racism**

Michael Huxley: **The Dancer's World, 1920–1945: Modern Dancers and Their Practices Reconsidered**

Michael Longo and Philomena Murray: **Europe's Legitimacy Crisis: From Causes to Solutions**

Mark Lauchs, Andy Bain and Peter Bell: **Outlaw Motorcycle Gangs: A Theoretical Perspective** palgrave▶pivot

Scaling the Tail: Managing Profitable Growth in Emerging Markets

Seung Ho Park

Gerardo R. Ungson

and

Andrew Cosgrove

palgrave
macmillan

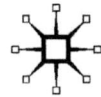

SCALING THE TAIL
Copyright © Seung Ho Park, Gerardo R. Ungson, and Andrew Cosgrove, 2015.
Foreword Copyright © John Quelch

All rights reserved.

First published in 2015 by
PALGRAVE MACMILLAN®
in the United States—a division of St. Martin's Press LLC,
175 Fifth Avenue, New York, NY 10010.

Where this book is distributed in the UK, Europe and the rest of the world, this is by Palgrave Macmillan, a division of Macmillan Publishers Limited, registered in England, company number 785998, of Houndmills, Basingstoke, Hampshire RG21 6XS.

Palgrave Macmillan is the global academic imprint of the above companies and has companies and representatives throughout the world.

Palgrave® and Macmillan® are registered trademarks in the United States, the United Kingdom, Europe and other countries.

ISBN: 978-1-137-53858-1 EPUB
ISBN: 978-1-137-53859-8 PDF
ISBN: 978-1-137-54353-0 Hardback

Library of Congress Cataloging-in-Publication Data is available from the Library of Congress.

A catalogue record of the book is available from the British Library.

First edition: 2015

www.palgrave.com/pivot

DOI: 10.1057/9781137538598

Contents

List of Boxes	vii
List of Figures	viii
List of Tables	x
Foreword *John Quelch*	xii
Acknowledgments	xiv

Part I   What Distinguishes Emerging Markets Today?

1	Introduction	2
2	Rethinking Conventional Models	10

Part II   Scaling the Tail: New Templates

3	Problematique	20
4	New Logics-Scaling the Tail	30

Part III   The "P-E-C" Framework

5	The Diagnostic "P-E-C" Framework	45
6	Positioning Firms for Profitable Growth	51
7	Defining the Drivers of Profitable Growth	67
8	Co-aligning Strategies with Management Structures and Systems	91

9	A Synthesis of Our Findings	108
10	Recommendations	120

Appendices	127
Bibliography	153
About the Authors	158
Index	160

List of Boxes

2.1	Testing the viability of four growth scenarios	12
3.1	Asia's emerging middle class	24
4.1	Contiguous interconnections—agglomeration as applied to this study	37
5.1	The P-E-C framework for achieving profitable growth-summary	48
7.1	Building synergy through localization and distribution at Want Want China Holdings Limited	72
7.2	Nestle's approach to multi-tiered branding	77
7.3	Learning in Malaysia's FNBM	81
7.4	Globalization and localization—when is too much or too little?	83
9.1	An interview with Ehab Abou Oaf	113

List of Figures

4.1	The progression of value-creation	32
6.1	Strategic objectives (current vs. in three years)	55
6.2	External drivers of firm strategy	56
6.3	Perceptions of market share changes	57
6.4	Sources of financial resources (current vs. in three years)	61
6.5	Perceptions of the significance of emerging markets	62
6.6	Expansion modes in emerging markets	63
6.7	Types of sales channels in emerging markets	64
7.1	Sources of competitive advantage in emerging markets	69
7.2	Drivers of revenue growth in emerging markets	74
7.3	Strategic focus on product categories	75
7.4	Strategies for product category development	76
7.5	Strategies for local brand positioning	81
7.6	Strategies for local product sourcing	82
7.7	Strategies for local product development	85
7.8	Strategies for local product sales	86
7.9	Strategies for local product distribution	86
7.10	Strategic drivers for cost reduction	87
8.1	The role of local management in business decisions	94
8.2	The localization of business activities	95
8.3	External barriers to profitable growth	97
8.4	Internal barriers to profitable growth	98

8.5	Strategies for building local management teams	100
8.6	Developing local strategic capabilities	102
8.7	Effectiveness of the local management team	106
9.1	The logic of "scaling the tail"	113
AIII.1	Parent firm global sales	144
AIII.2	Subsidiary local sales	144
AIII.3	Country representation of survey sample	145
AIII.4	Industry representation of survey sample	145
AIII.5	Respondents by job titles	146

List of Tables

2.1	Growth trajectories	13
2.2	Why traditional scaling up fails—obstacles and barriers	16
3.1	Conventional strategies and core assumptions	22
3.2	Changes in inflection points	26
4.1	The long tail and scaling the tail: implications for emerging markets (EM)	36
4.2	Scales, definitions, examples, and implications	40
6.1	Differentiating higher and lower performing firms in positioning	65
7.1	Differentiating higher and lower performing firms in positioning	88
7.2	Differentiating higher and lower performing firms in drivers	89
8.1	Differentiating higher and lower performing firms in co-alignment	107
9.1	Conventional entry strategies versus emerging strategic templates	111
9.2	The P-E-C diagnostic framework and strategic drivers	112
AI.1	Participants in the field study	128
AII.1	Survey question 1	130
AII.2	Survey question 2	130
AII.3	Survey question 3	131
AII.4	Survey question 4	131
AII.5	Survey question 5	131
AII.6	Survey question 7	132

AII.7	Survey question 8	133
AII.8	Survey question 10	134
AII.9	Survey question 14	135
AII.10	Survey question 15	136
AII.11	Survey question 18	137
AII.12	Survey question 24	139
AII.13	Survey question 25	139
AII.14	Survey question 28	141
AII.15	Survey question 29	141
AII.16	Survey question 30	142
AIV.1	Sales growth for the overall sample	147
AIV.2	Profitability for the overall sample	148
AIV.3	Sales growth for foreign firms	149
AIV.4	Profitability for foreign firms	149
AIV.5	Sales growth for profitable growth firms	151
AIV.6	Profitability for profitable growth firms	151
AIV.7	List of profitable growth companies	151

Foreword

In emerging markets, the adage "the only constant is change" is self-evident. The tried-and-true strategies that multinational companies have used in emerging markets are no longer working. What the world has witnessed is nothing short of a complete revolution in the requirements for success in emerging markets. Local markets are no longer easy and fertile ground in which major multinationals can enter and flourish on auto-pilot. Local companies have recognized the threat of the immense resources and economies of scale possessed by major multinational corporations. In response, local companies have appealed more specifically and effectively to local customers, a task for which they are uniquely qualified. Of course, the owners, employees, and marketing strategies of these local companies are typically from the country and culture of interest. From this perspective, it is understandable that a "one-size-fits-all" approach would eventually fail on a large scale. In fact, it could be argued that multinational companies could be grateful that their generic strategies have worked for as long as they could in emerging markets. However, what are they to do now?

This book appears at a crucial inflexion point in the fate of multinational corporations in consumer goods and retailing sectors. It provides right answers to the following two core questions: (1) Why are so many major multinational companies failing in emerging markets? and (2) Exactly what actions can these and other companies take to succeed in these radically changed environments? To answer these questions, under the auspices of a collaborative team involving EY and the Economist Intelligence Unit, the authors have conducted in-depth field interviews, along with a survey of 253 managers across 10 countries. From these data, they present a model that prescribes the specific actions that multinational companies can take to compete effectively with local companies and sustain profitable growth.

Scaling the Tail: Managing Profitable Growth in Emerging Markets presents an important means. Companies will fail or prosper depending on whether or not they understand the current situation and take the suggestions made in this book. Companies that follow its prescriptions should enjoy profitable growth that exceeds what they achieved when their "one-size-fits-all" strategies were still appropriate. Cost-effective customization rather than cost-efficient standardization should guide the strategies of multinational corporations.

John Quelch
Harvard Business School

Acknowledgments

It is well recognized that examining even a small handful of emerging markets can be a daunting task. To this end, we acknowledge the invaluable partnership with the EY Consumer Group, notably the assistance of Emmanuelle Roman and Nicola Gates. The team arranged for the initial field interviews with the leading global managers of EY. We worked together with them in designing, vetting, and revising the survey questionnaire. Through their contacts, the Economist Intelligence Unit was contracted to administer the survey to 276 managers in 10 countries.

EY has published its own report, *Profit-or-Lose: Balancing the Growth-Profit Paradox for Global Consumer Products Companies and Retailers in Asia's Emerging Markets*, EYG no. EN0519; CSG/GSC2013/1164313; ED 1015. This report details the analysis of the survey, interviews, and recommendations. Because EY has its own focus of interest that might not necessarily coincide with this book, we highly recommend a reading of this companion report.

We acknowledge a special debt to Dr. Nan Zhou, formerly a Research Fellow of the Institute for Emerging Market Studies (IEMS). As a coauthor of our earlier book *Rough Diamonds: the Four Successful Traits of Breakout Firms in BRIC Countries*, she participated in cradling the topic of profitable growth when she was with IEMS. In this study, she participated in some of the field interviews, conducted the case studies, supervised the student assistants, and undertook the initial analysis and presentation of the survey results.

We extend special thanks to managers who participated in this study, either through IEMS or EY, including Rob

Mitchell and Mariko Asao. We are also greatly indebted to two of our friends, Anthony Tsai and Ehab Abou Oaf. Anthony worked for P&G for decades before moving to Beijing Hualian, a leading Chinese retailer, to lead its innovation center and marketing activities in China. Ehab, currently Asia Pacific President of Mars Chocolate, was also part of P&G's international operations for over a decade before he joined Mars Chocolate in 2000. They have had the daunting task of managing global leading retail companies across many different countries in Eastern Europe and Asia. Their experiences and knowledge on emerging markets played a pivotal role in forming the core idea of this book. They allowed hours of multiple interviews and feedback as we were formulating our thoughts and ideas for this book.

We acknowledge the use of company documents, websites, and field interviews as our source and basis of ensuing observations and arguments. If a specific secondary source is used, however, it is acknowledged as an endnote. We would like to thank the following research assistants and students who helped with the research and compile information about the companies included in this book: Ji Hong, Liu Wen, Chinmay Ojha, and Urvashi Prasad. We are grateful for the generous funding and support from the Research Center for Emerging Market Studies of China Europe International Business School and the International Business Department of San Francisco State University. Special thanks also go to Michael O'Brien for assisting the research, Yim-Yu Wong, and Linda Oubre, San Francisco State University, for overall support. We also thank Karl Johansson, Jay Nibbie, Uschi Schreiber, and other global leaders of EY for their support and appreciation of research projects and activities on emerging markets.

Finally, as with most ongoing studies, family time can be restrictive. In this context, we deeply thank our families for their patience and support: Ja Young, Alexandra, and Amelia; Suki, Tanya, Mark, Tegan, Boden Kai, Carlo, Kaipo, Matt, Rainelle, Max, and Daisy; and to Amanda, Cameron, and Max.

palgrave▶pivot

www.palgrave.com/pivot

Part I
What Distinguishes Emerging Markets Today?

1
Introduction

Abstract: *This chapter provides an overview of our core arguments. Although profitable growth is widely acclaimed, there are differences on how to approach it. Traditional strategies for emerging markets emphasize entering large and undifferentiated markets, recalibrating products to make them more attractive and affordable for targeted segments, and capitalizing on economies of scale and scope to reduce overall costs. Our research indicates that this approach is limited, if not misplaced, when addressing the emerging needs of affluent middle-class sectors. An alternative logic focuses on building mass sales at the periphery of the distribution using broad differentiation strategies. This is developed with select partners as an overarching theme throughout the book and supported by field interviews and a survey of consumer goods in select Asian countries.*

Park, Seung Ho, Gerardo R. Ungson, and Andrew Cosgrove. *Scaling the Tail: Managing Profitable Growth in Emerging Markets.* New York: Palgrave Macmillan, 2015. DOI: 10.1057/9781137538598.0008.

Introduction

Profitable growth is a term in good currency. It is increasingly recognized as a powerful concept to describe sustained competitive advantage in market economies. After all, a firm that consistently posts high profits and sales growth over an extended period is considered to be the gold standard in both developed and emerging markets.

From previous studies, the strategy for achieving profitable growth in emerging markets has been the time-tested mantra employed by successful multinationals: enter large and relatively untapped mass consumption markets, recalibrate products to make them more affordable for these targeted segments, capitalize on economies of scale and scope, bring experts from the home country and hire local talent, and develop formidable supply chains to assure efficient distribution. The logic is simple: unleash the full power of a business model geared toward achieving market dominance through products that are affordably priced and reaping high profits through high volume sales over time.

But, as this book will detail, this strategy has not been effective as of late. The key problems include stronger local competition, difficulty in scaling up operations, failure to overcome the high transaction costs, inability to secure proper logistics and distribution, intensity of foreign competitors, unsupportive government regulations, and unanticipated responses by targeted affluent consumers to commodity offerings. All of these were underestimated by many multinational firms that adhered to the old practice of providing lower-priced commodities in mass consumption markets on a large scale.

What precipitated this change in outcomes? Why does the strategy that had worked so well in the past is largely ineffective in this current context? The failure to adapt is not due to a lack of resolve, nor is it the absence of strategic intent or good intentions. It arises from a significant shift in the market environment that has reduced the efficacy of a large scope—low-cost strategy. This problem is particularly manifest in strategies that attempt to capture market share from the fast-growing yet previously nascent segments, most notably the middle-class sectors in emerging markets, particularly in the BRIC (Brazil, Russia, India, and China) countries. Specifically, the wellspring of new market niches has created an uneven level of economic development that is clustered in different cities and regions, a context that McKinsey has ascribed the popular moniker "granular growth."[1] In a global context, this disparity between high and low growth and development has been referred to as a "multispeed" world.[2] In this study, we argue that new consumption preferences by these fast-developing market sectors do not align well with the established practice of mass consumption applied to merchandising.

As will be detailed in this book, the evolving state of these preferences has led to what appear to be paradoxical, even conflicting, imperatives and modalities. These changing patterns call into question whether mass consumption lodged in the logic of manufacturing applies to the unmet needs and expectations of an emerging middle class. Likewise, this raises new challenges within emerging markets as to whether a single strategic approach to profitable growth is still appropriate, or whether multiple strategies oriented at mainstream and peripheral products have become the new norm.

In all, these recent developments prompt answers to several new questions. What new characteristics of the changing competitive landscape warrant more detailed attention? How can current and aspiring firms position themselves in this new environment? What new strategic templates should be adopted, and what should be discarded? How can a firm respond more effectively to surging market niches in the context of granular growth?

Clearly, a new business model is needed, but what type of model?

Framing a new business model

This book presents a different model of profitable growth, "scaling the tail," that extends recent theoretical advances in value-creation. It has long been asserted that mass sales occur at the center of the statistical (normal) distribution, while sales in the periphery (or the tail) are regarded as fragmented and less significant. In a provocative reformulation, Chris Anderson (*The Long Tail*) reversed this logic by arguing that peripheral sales now outnumber traditional mass sales, primarily because digital technology has changed the economics of how goods are produced, stored, sold, and distributed, giving rise to the term "the long tail."[3] Even so, sales at the long tail, while large in the aggregate, remain fragmented and episodic.

For close to two years, researchers from the Institute of Emerging Market Studies (IEMS),[4] working in tandem with a counterpart group from EY, deliberated on the subject of profitable growth. Our discussions led to several in-depth interviews with leading global managers from different emerging markets in Asia, principally to better understand the dynamics of profitable growth. However, because our conclusions regarding the "scaling of the long tail" were still preliminary and based mainly on the experiences of highly successful firms, IEMS and EY designed a cross-sectional survey of 276 managers in 10 emerging markets with a wider performance range. The ensuing study was conducted under the auspices of a collaborative EY team and the Economist Intelligence Unit. Collectively, the data form the basis for our ensuing arguments and reformulations.

Placed in the context of a total argument, our extension of current theory advances the following thesis: sales in the periphery are not simply aggregated, but they are *contiguously interconnected* as well, leading to scaling effects of their own. This condition is particularly evident in the branding strategy of the consumer goods and retailing sectors that targeted fast-developing sectors, such as the middle class in emerging markets. We term this "scaling the tail."

In building the case for "scaling the tail" through interconnectedness, as opposed to simple aggregation, we provide fine-grained insights into how performance by firms in the consumer goods and retailing sectors[5] is differentiated by their abilities to nurture specialized market niches using high-end brands, flank particular segments with multiproducts, build synergies from product categories, manage granular growth, develop deeply nuanced localization strategies, and install performance-based cultures with supportive management systems.

On the basis of these considerations, a prescriptive framework—the P (positioning), E (exploring strategic drivers), and C (co-aligning management systems)—was formulated to further guide our inquiry about profitable growth. In these deliberations, "scaling the tail" constituted the overarching theoretical anchor. This framework became the organizing logic for subsequent analysis of the cross-sectional survey and for synthesizing our findings with our earlier interviews.

For perspective, this chapter provides an overview of the entire study, highlighting key findings and conclusions. Chapter 2 reviews developments relating to profitable growth in emerging markets, culling from the established literature, including those from our earlier work (*Rough Diamonds*). Chapter 3 brings to the fore the specific challenges and questions arising out of unresolved questions and issues from established research. We also discuss key changes in the external environment with an emphasis on the middle-class sectors in emerging markets, which led to defining new inflection points that change the directionality of a strategy. In Chapter 4, we formally introduce the main theoretical components of a new business model ("scaling the tail") that proposes a progression of value-creation within the lifecycles of product innovations. Chapter 5 introduces and builds further on the organizing logic of the "P-E-C" framework, which was used to guide and organize our findings and conclusions from the field survey. The next three chapters (Chapters 6–8) present our survey findings and insights from the interviews that delineate differences between higher and lower performing firms in their positioning strategies, their competitive drivers to achieve advantage, and the co-alignment of their management structures and processes with their strategies. In all, these chapters present suggestions for selecting high niche markets, defining strategic drivers and scaling opportunities, and elucidating the focal points motivating investment decisions and the cues for building a resilient profit-oriented organizational culture. The final two chapters (Chapters 9–10) present our overall conclusions and recommendations for multinational firms in emerging markets to attain profitable growth.

Our interest in profitable growth began in parallel with an initial project (*Rough Diamonds*) that detailed exemplary breakout firms in the BRIC countries.[6] In this work that spanned five years, the IEMS team identified and examined breakout firms that had previously been shielded from the popular press and the academic limelight, but that could become the foundation for sustained growth in emerging markets. Our primary interest lies in understanding the differences between these newly emerging leading local firms and foreign multinationals from developed countries.

This book complements our earlier work in its focus on foreign multinational firms that are currently operating in emerging markets. Admittedly, there is a considerable body of work in this area, one that has constituted the bulk of international business. Nevertheless, this study is among the first to examine activities in the context of fast-developing middle-class sectors in emerging markets. Although this rise has been anticipated, few, if any work, have focused on the direct consequences of emergent affluence of the middle class on corporate strategies and management systems.

Even so, offering popular brand items through multi-branding and brand extensions is hardly a novel strategy. This has been practiced, if not perfected, by leading companies, such as Procter and Gamble, Colgate-Palmolive, Nike, Unilever, and others for decades, but mostly in developed markets. What distinguishes this application in emerging markets is the attention placed on the surging expectations and preferences of the middle class, along with our arguments for agglomeration. Some core arguments relating to this particular application include the following:

- Conventional strategic thinking based on mass sales differs from "scaling the tail" not merely in application, but in its underlying logic. The economics of cost leadership based on manufacturing are different from the strategy of differentiation based on brand extensions and multibranding. Yet, in scaling and growth decisions, firms tend to treat the two logics similarly, leading to erroneous assumptions in application.
- Growth in emerging markets is indeed faster than developed markets. However, growth is also unbalanced and uneven, confirming some experts' view that growth is granular,[7] with consequences on how to select untapped market segments.
- Scaling is achieved not by simply aggregating market sales, but through a strategy of contiguous interconnectedness, or building intangible "mental" linkages between similar brands that are predicated on network effects.
- Multibrands are needed to flank segments, but not in the manner typically understood in developed markets, which is to secure shelf space and protect the major brands. Instead, multibranding is needed to provide multiple options and accommodate a relatively "insecure" consumer who is neither price-conscious nor brand-loyal. Hence, multi-branding is employed to scale up product categories in particular market segments.
- Localization is typically understood in terms of refining a standard product, oftentimes trimming down features, to make the product affordable to local markets. Our study indicates that this is no longer the case. Localization extends beyond product/marketing embellishments to mean investment in local talent, the market sector, and even the community.
- While localization is generally favored by pundits, there is the risk of overlocalizing that could lead to high transferable costs. Localization is not any single event or decision, but rather a process. Profitable growth entails tempering local needs through systemic learning.

- It is more widely acknowledged that multinational corporations (MNCs) need to move beyond expat management to hiring locals. However, this is not enough; to succeed, MNCs have to nurture and develop local talent.
- Higher and lower performing firms differ in terms of their perceptions of the environment, their attributions of local strengths, their dependency on corporate headquarters, their approach to building local teams, and their investment decisions.
- Building a profit-oriented culture hardly comes through self-acclamation, but is the result of consistent investments and decentralization of decisions to the local units, as well as developing and investing in supportive management systems and processes.

In all, we provide specific implications for MNCs in the consumer goods and retailing industries, as these relate to profitable growth. In our assessment, a new strategic template based on more incisive interpretations of scaling might be appropriate to the fast-changing competitive landscape of emerging markets.

Accordingly, we envision three types of audiences for our book. The first audience would be academicians in the areas of international business, strategy, management, and marketing. In addition to delving into the subject matter of each field, the extension of Anderson's "long tail" might be informative, and hopefully compelling, in addressing new forms of value-creation in today's world. The second audience comprises business practitioners who typically seek new templates for understanding the changes in emerging markets and strategies to respond to them. Relatedly, the third audience is management/strategy consultants who are interested in new insights about emerging markets, and possibly new templates that can enrich their basic advocacy.

Notes

1. Patrick Viguerie, Sven Smit, and Mehrdad Baghai, *The Granularity of Growth* (Hoboken, NJ: John Wiley & Sons, 2008).
2. See Michael Spence, *The Next Convergence: The Future of Economic Growth in a Multispeed World* (New York: Farrar, Straus and Giroux, 2011). Unlike the McKinsey formulation that focuses on intracountry development, Spence examines the disparities between countries and economic blocs.
3. Chris Anderson, *The Long Tail: Why the Future of Business Is Selling Less of More* (New York: Hyperion, 2006). Since its publication, there has been a flurry of

contested claims about the efficacy of the long tail. In our adaptation, we do not argue that sales in the center of the distribution are insignificant, particularly when applied to commodity markets, but that scaling can occur in previously nascent, but developing, market niches, such as the middle class.

4 The research team consisted of Park, Ungson, and Zhou. Numerous students were also hired as research assistants to develop templates for firms to be interviewed. In the following chapters, we adopted the following stylistic format: IEMS team refers to Park, Ungson, Zhou, and other research assistants, while "we," "our," or "us" refer to Park and Ungson.

5 Although this might appear to be limiting, these industries are large and prominent in emerging markets, as they are in developed economies. This category includes beauty and health products, personal products, adult and baby foods, snacks, detergents, among others. These industries were among those recommended by EY's global managers in the initial interviews.

6 Seung Ho Park, Nan Zhou, and Gerardo R. Ungson, *Rough Diamonds: The Four Successful Traits of Breakout Firms in BRIC Countries* (San Francisco, CA: Jossey Bass, 2013). In this study, exemplary firms, or "rough diamonds," were evaluated on multiple financial measures, including profitability, sales growth, and efficiency. In all, they outpace comparable groups and have grown at an average rate of 43% over 10 years; in other words, they double their sales every 1.9 years.

7 Yuval Atsmon, Michael Kloss, and Sven Smit, "Parsing the growth advantage of emerging-market companies." *McKinsey Quarterly* (May 2012); M. Baghai, S. Smit, and P. Viguerie, "The granularity of growth." *McKinsey Quarterly* (2007).

2
Rethinking Conventional Models

Abstract: *In this chapter, we discuss and appraise conventional entry strategies and their underlying assumptions. Findings from a broad sample of firms (n=105,260 firms operating in the BRIC nations) indicate that firms pursuing high sales growth are less successful than firms focused on profitability. Moreover, firms that started with a high growth strategy were less likely to achieve profitable growth over time compared to firms with the goal of profitability. We review possible reasons why scaling based on the logic of mass consumption for commodities is not effective. We underscore the need to explore fine-grained expectations of middle-class consumers, and argue for profitable growth based on a different type of scaling. Cases highlight the successful experiences of firms operating in China and India.*

Park, Seung Ho, Gerardo R. Ungson, and Andrew Cosgrove. *Scaling the Tail: Managing Profitable Growth in Emerging Markets.* New York: Palgrave Macmillan, 2015. DOI: 10.1057/9781137538598.0009.

An earlier study on the common features of breakout firms from emerging markets (*Rough Diamonds: The Four Successful Traits of Breakout Firms in BRIC Countries*) established the conditions in which these firms posted high profits and high sales growth over an extended time period.[1] We had argued that the succession of exemplary new firms exhibiting profitable growth, specifically called "rough diamonds," provides a complementary way of appraising the development and transformation of emerging markets, both within the BRICs and extending to prospering emerging markets. This emphasis on the microfoundation of successive and generational firm success over time contrasts with standard measures of macroeconomic growth at the country level, which have characterized earlier studies of the BRICs.[2]

Historically, there have been numerous academic studies and consulting reports that have provided frameworks to assess how firms achieve high profits over time.[3] This is hardly surprising, given the salience and centrality of the topic. In fact, sustainable competitive advantage forms the bedrock of strategic management research.[4] On the basis of this work, it is now widely acknowledged that high performing firms sustain their advantage by formulating a clearly articulated formal strategy, an understanding of competitors and the external environment, astute competitive positioning, and supportive management systems.

Because much of academic research was developed in advanced economies, its application to emerging markets prompts additional questions: Might there be differences between developed and emerging markets that influence strategic choices? What distinguishes successful from less successful firms? What might be the relative advantages of multinational corporations (MNCs) compared to those of local firms? To what extent should localization be pursued? Will it make a difference whether firms initially pursued profitability or sales growth?

Testing the viability of growth scenarios

As a backdrop to these questions, in an earlier study, we examined a broad sample of firms (n=105,260 from the BRIC nations),[5] specifically comparing firms that initially pursued sales growth or profitability. Of course, most firms do both; the issue was where their primary emphasis might be at the outset. Our initial expectation was that firms, regardless of their choice of initial performance measures, would eventually find the appropriate path to profitable growth. Even so, after delineating two distinct time periods for analysis, we found that firms that had initially opted for high sales growth were less likely to attain profitable growth over time. In fact, almost 42% of these companies fell into the low-growth and low-profit status in the following period, while around 15% of the profit-oriented firms failed. In contrast, the chances were much higher for the profit-oriented companies to achieve profitable growth later than the growth-oriented companies (35% vs. 9.5 %, respectively; see Box 2.1).

BOX 2.1 *Testing the viability of four growth scenarios*

To validate the presence of four types of growth, we compiled firm data in key sectors (including industrial goods, consumer products, financial services, energy and utility, technology, media, transportation, infrastructure, and life science) in each of the BRIC countries from the period 2002 to 2011, totaling 105,260 firms. From the data, we determined that the initial decisions made by these firms relating to how to grow, either through sales or profits, depend upon their intent and circumstances. The overarching question of this research is: Which path leads to sustained growth over time?

To examine performance, we divided the time period into two phases: Phase I (2002–2006) and Phase II (2007–2011), and classified firms in each phase into four scenarios: high sales growth/ high profit (HH), high sales growth/low profit (HL), low sales growth/high profit (LH), and low sales growth/low profit (LL). High or low sales growth and profit is determined by using the average industry sales growth and profit during each phase as the baseline.

We then tracked the transition of firms in terms of the four cells. Which strategy has a better prospect of leading to profitable growth in emerging markets? Table 2.1 summarizes the growth trajectories in these two stages.

TABLE 2.1 *Growth trajectories*

Phase I (2002–2006) Status	Phase II (2007–2011) HH (%)	Phase II (2007–2011) HL (%)	Phase II (2007–2011) LH (%)	Phase II (2007–2011) LL (%)
High sales/high profit (profitable growth), HH	36.7	16.9	31.1	15.3
High sales/low profit (sales-oriented strategy), HL	9.5	40.5	8.4	41.6
Low sales/high profit (profit-oriented strategy), LH	35.3	13.2	36.2	15.3
Low sales/low profit, LL	11.5	34.3	10.8	43.5

The table reveals different patterns for sustaining performance. For firms that started with high sales growth and high profits, they are likely to maintain such a level over time (36.7%), and sustain high profits even with low sales growth (31.1%). Of interest are the firms that pursued high sales growth or high profits. For sales-growth-oriented firms, only 9.5% are able to achieve profitable growth over time and are likely to fail (41.6%). In contrast, firms that pursued high profits are more likely to achieve profitable growth (35.3%) and have less likelihood of failing over time (15.3%). The data suggest an initial profit-oriented strategy has better prospects of leading to both high sales growth and profits in the future than an initial sales growth strategy.

Source: Excerpted from Seung Ho Park, Nan Zhou, and Gerardo R. Ungson, *Rough Diamonds: The Four Traits of Successful Breakout Firms in BRIC Countries* (San Francisco: Jossey Bass, 2013), pp. 112–124.

Because this finding did not support some well-established logic and beliefs, we reexamined the underlying assumptions about profitable growth as applied to emerging economies. Specifically, in the PIMS (Profit Impact on Marketing Strategy) Study, which is considered to be the authoritative work on the relationship between profits and market share, it is postulated that gaining market share over time, conceivably by pursuing high sales growth, would eventually redound to higher profitability. Presumably, lower unit or variable costs would arise from economies of scale and scope.[6] While profits might be low at the initial stages because of a lower price point, as might be the case of a commodity product, lower unit costs would eventually offset this price-cost disadvantage, and higher profit margins would ensue over time. Moreover, firms with a large market share (or industries with high concentration) were in a position to influence the basis of competition.[7] In all, the prevailing logic is that large market scope would lead to broad cost and/or differentiation advantages.

In the case of our sample of firms from the BRICs, however, this pattern was *not* upheld. In fact, the opposite direction was observed, that is, those firms that initially opted for high sales growth were much more vulnerable to experiencing lower profit performance over time. In contrast, firms that pursued high profitability were more likely to attain profitable growth over time. Moreover, the type of industry did not appear to matter. This pattern was observed for firms operating in commodity and differentiated markets. These firms that pursued sales growth failed to expand in a manner that led to significant market share. These findings prompted several questions. Why is this so? Does this pattern describe the general experiences of firms in emerging markets? Does this abrogate conventional wisdom about competing in emerging markets?

Why scaling does not work in this new environment

To answer these questions, we initiated a number of field interviews with global managers in the consumer goods and retailing sectors, all situated in Asia. These managers were carefully selected and considered to be among Asia's top thought leaders by IEMS. In our interviews, managers elaborated on the new requirements and contexts for profitable growth to occur. Developing large mass markets, whether for purposes of production or consumption, is inextricably related to economies of large scale and scope. When economies are realized, scaling up is a formidable strategic weapon. Historically, large-sized MNCs, many of which started small, achieved dominance once they were able to scale up to broad markets and attain economies of scale and scope. Harvard strategy professor Michael Porter proposed three main generic strategies, that is, cost leadership, differentiation, and focus that provide firms with tangible competitive advantages using appropriate scaling.[8]

As applied to emerging markets, however, scaling up is currently much more difficult than was previously the case. Anthony Tsai, a former Procter & Gamble manager for decades and the general manager of Beijing Hualian Hypermarket Ltd., recounts his experience: "The previous model of growth employed by Unilever and P & G that sought to scale up manufacturing and marketing facilities did not work as well in China because of sheer logistical difficulties."

Emerging markets are typically characterized by geographically fragmented markets and by concentrated sectors that are difficult to access due to poor marketing channels and inadequate physical infrastructure. Harvard professors Tarun Khanna and Krishnan Palepu call this lack of market-facilitating mechanisms "institutional voids."[9] These voids increase start-up and operating costs. This condition was initially observed in faulted strategies to penetrate the "bottom of the pyramid," but has since been extended to cover most emerging and developing markets.[10] Conventional logic dictates that different products, most with trimmed-down features, be positioned to capitalize on such segments, although the advocacy to address the bottom of the pyramid still remains in its infancy stage. Nevertheless, the preponderance of action is still focused on servicing large and accessible mainstream markets with affordable products.

Tsai contends that scaling up manufacturing facilities to reduce costs makes sense in a production-centric environment, but is less compelling in a marketing or merchandising (retail) environment where differentiated product features are desired. Even when manufacturing scaling is possible, firms have faced additional difficulties in selling products. In the past, this was less of a problem because the products comprise commodities, in which there is less branding and where price constitutes the critical factor. In marketing or merchandising settings, however, products are not necessarily commodities.

According to Anthony Tsai, more affluent consumers are much less attracted to lower priced items than they were previously. Accordingly, a firm has to invest further in assuring that the mass-produced product is affordable and acceptable to the targeted consumers. If these costs are significant, they increase the transactional costs to a level that is not offset by other cost reductions that arise from scaling. As one example, the US electronic store Best Buy faced serious adversity in China when its broad product offerings in retail stores across the country were not well accepted by Chinese consumers. Moreover, the company did not fare well against local competitors. Ultimately, these led to the closure of Best Buy stores in China in 2011.[11] As we will discuss later in this report, the growth and sophistication of an emerging affluent middle class raise a far different consumption mindset than their counterparts in developed economies.

Ehab Abou Oaf, Asia-Pacific president of Mars Chocolate, a world renowned manufacturer of chocolate bars and products, also worked for P & G for ten years before joining Mars in 2000. He notes that China, in particular, has been growing fast, with rates approaching 15–20%, although chocolate sales have been increasing as well in Taiwan, Thailand, Vietnam, and the Philippines. For Ehab, the sophistication of consumers depends in large part on where they reside. In the top 40 cities in China, specifically, sales have soared. However, he also noted difficulties in scaling up sales to other cities. Scaling, he opines, depends on the impact of several variables—imports, logistics, nontariff barriers, and the ability of hiring and retaining talent. Moreover, because consumers in these different cities have different tastes and purchasing power, it is a mistake to simply offer a standardized, "one-size-fits-all" type of product. Hence, to sustain sales, the firm must understand the deep-seated preferences of their multi-faceted consumers. Without the margins from scale and/or scope economies, it is impossible to effectively implement broad cost leadership or differentiation strategies. Given these characteristics of emerging markets, traditional scaling can be limited and ineffective (Table 2.2).[12]

For many failed MNCs, the inability to scale up was either underestimated, or simply missed entirely.[13] They were operating well within the

TABLE 2.2 *Why traditional scaling up fails—obstacles and barriers*

1. Institutional voids, specifically the lack of adequate infrastructure and market intermediaries, raise the costs of scaling up and geographic expansion.
2. Even with adequate scaling, there might be inadequate demand and the absence of purchasing power needed to absorb the increased volume of products and services. However, even when purchasing power is present, consumers might not purchase the lower priced items, which they regard as exhibiting low quality.
3. Diseconomies of scale can result from significantly higher localization costs, administrative complexity, and the lack of control/coordination mechanisms.
4. There can be a backlash against MNC expansion activities in some geographical quarters.

   Taken collectively, scaling up is not guaranteed, nor can it be assumed to be efficient. Moreover, affordability is important as assumed by the business model, but compatibility between the product/services and targeted consumers might be as consequential.

parameters of previous business models that had once worked, but did not resonate with the emerging changes in the competitive landscape. The logic of scaling in manufacturing did not translate as well as scaling in marketing or merchandising (retail).

What accounts for this misplaced assumption? Understandably, international firms decry the lack of good information about emerging markets as a major problem.[14] Without a thorough understanding of the changing trends in competition and consumer tastes, a firm can blindly follow an existing growth strategy that would lead to disappointing market performance. After a second round of field interviews with top managers selected in collaboration with EY, it was apparent that a profound change was underway in emerging markets. The competitive environment had ushered in a wave of new local competitors, but more importantly, a change in consumer expectations and requirements. But what precisely is the context of this new environment? How has the logic of competition changed?

These contravening issues compelled a closer examination of extant models, and their core assumptions and predictions. We searched more deeply for explanations about why scaling had failed to materialize. We examined precipitating factors, notably the rise and the impact of the middle class, which had led to these changes. Collectively, these issues are discussed in our next chapter.

Notes

1. S. H. Park, N. Zhou, and G. R. Ungson, *Rough Diamonds: The Four Successful Traits of Breakout Firms in BRIC Countries* (San Francisco, CA: Jossey Bass, 2013).
2. See, in particular, "Dreaming with BRICs: the path to 2050" (Goldman Sachs, 2003) and "Coming of age" (*Economist*, January 2006) that trumpeted the arrival of emerging economies. More recent publications are Jim O'Neil, *The Growth Map: Economic Opportunity in the BRICs and Beyond* (New York: Portfolio/Penguin, 2011) and Ruchir Sharma, *Breakout Nations: In Pursuit of the Next Economic Miracles* (New York: W. W. Norton, 2012). While both studies include other measures, such as institutional development, the primary indicator is macroeconomic growth at the country level.
3. Deloitte & Touche (2011) "In pursuit of profitable growth: restructuring an operating model for emerging markets; EY (2012) "Rethinking profitable growth: the productivity imperative for foreign multinationals in China"; Pricewaterhouse Coopers (2012); "Profitable growth strategies for the global emerging middle: learning from the 'next 4 billion' markets."

4 While there are many excellent textbooks on strategic management, a good introductory primer is Thomas L. Wheelan and J. David Unger, *Strategic Management and Business Policy* (Upper Saddle River, NJ: Prentice Hall, 2006).
5 This section is excerpted from our previous work, *Rough Diamonds*, pp. 112–124.
6 The findings discussed in this section are based on R. D. Buzzell and B. T. Gale, *The PIMS Principles: Linking Strategy to Performance* (New York: Free Press, 1987). For a reassessment, see P. Farris, M. J. Moore, and R. Buzzell, *The Profit Impact of Marketing Strategy Project: Retrospect and Prospects* (Cambridge: Cambridge University Press, 2004).
7 R. D. Buzzell and B. T. Gale, *The PIMS Principles*. P. Farris, M. J. Moore and R. Buzzell, *The Profit Impact of Marketing Strategy Project*. Also see F. T. Knickerbocker, "Oligopolistic reaction and multinational enterprise," *International Executive*, 1973. 15(2):7–9.
8 For a good discussion on cost leadership and product differentiation, see Michael E. Porter, *Competitive Strategy* (New York: Free Press, 1980).
9 Tarun Khanna and Krishna Palepu, *Winning in Emergent Markets: A Roadmap for Strategy and Execution* (Boston, MA: Harvard Business School Publishing, 2010).
10 Jamie Anderson and Costas Markides, "Strategic innovation at the base of the pyramid," *MIT Sloan Management Review*, Fall 2007. 49(1):83–88.
11 Example drawn from John Quelch and Katherine Jocz, *All Business Is Local: Why Place Matters More Than Ever in a Global, Virtual World* (New York: Portfolio/Penguin, 2012), p. 212.
12 While analysts attribute various reasons why these firms failed to realize their goals, a common attribute is the difficulty in scaling. For additional background on how firms can adjust to recent developments in emerging markets, see M. F. Letelier, F. Flores, and C. Spinosa, "Developing productive consumers in emerging markets," *California Management Review*, 45(4):77–103. Product No. CMR263, 2003.; and S. Shankar, C. Ormiston, N. Bloch, R. Schaus, and V. Vishwanath, "How to win in emerging markets," *MIT Sloan Management Review*, 49 (3):18–24. Product No. 49309, 2008; "Backlash against multinationals," *Economics Help*, August 2008. http://econ.economicshelp.org/2008/08/backlash-against-multinationals.html.
13 John Quelch and Katherine Jocz, *All Business Is Local: Why Place Matters More Than Ever in a Global, Virtual World* (New York: Portfolio/Penguin, 2012), p. 212.
14 Monitoring Services, "Over 50% of global companies fail to make emerging markets information readily available for staff." Read more at http://www.globalintelligence.com/insights-analysis/bulletins/over-50-of-global-companies-fail-to-make-emerging-#ixzz2Rb8pQnrg.

Part II

Scaling the Tail:
New Templates

3
Problematique

Abstract: *Historically, scaling for mass markets worked when emerging markets were characterized as low-cost-sourcing destinations, when commodities were the end product, and when local competition was insignificant. In the current environment, affluent middle-class sectors in emerging markets are found to have different consumption patterns, tend to be more brand-conscious, but can also be less secure in their preferences. Local competitors have bolstered their abilities to attend to these segments. Without changing mindsets, MNCs have experienced difficulties in mass merchandising strategies in emerging markets. Using illustrations and case studies, the chapter discusses inflection points that depict a shift from cost-driven to demand-enhancing competition. Instead of a logic based on mass manufacturing, attention has been directed at entering propitious market niches based on broad differentiation strategies.*

Park, Seung Ho, Gerardo R. Ungson, and Andrew Cosgrove. *Scaling the Tail: Managing Profitable Growth in Emerging Markets.* New York: Palgrave Macmillan, 2015. DOI: 10.1057/9781137538598.0011.

With much of the developed world mired in deep economic stagnation, there is much anticipation over the prospects of emerging markets. Even so, such markets are both a blessing and a curse. On the one hand, emerging markets are projected to grow at a significantly higher level than developed markets primarily because (1) they have a larger demographic base for future consumers; (2) they manifest a surging and growing affluent middle class; and (3) they have had a historically efficient (low cost) platform for manufacturing and outsourcing activities. And yet, these same markets are characterized by relatively underdeveloped institutions, broad geographical markets, fragmented market segments, insufficient market facilitating mechanisms and incentives, and relatively poor governance systems.[1]

Conventional thinking and core assumptions

In response to rising costs in their home countries, multinational corporations (MNCs) sought out suitable countries that had lower labor costs as destinations for building large volume manufacturing plants. Conventional wisdom was that these firms could gain a cost advantage and that products manufactured in these countries could be sold broadly in traditional developed markets. This gave rise to a dominant cost mentality and production-centric logic.

With the growing affluence of developing countries as consumer markets, not necessarily as manufacturing sites, it is not all surprising that this production-centric logic still remains prevalent. Specifically, emerging markets are now regarded as sizeable markets for mass consumption goods that complement MNCs' manufacturing activities. To illustrate, thoughtful commentators extol the need to "enter the mass market to achieve scale in distribution, brand building and operations."[2]

The core elements of this mass consumption strategy are presented in Table 3.1, along with some underlying assumptions about consumers in emerging markets. The overarching logic is to enter large markets for mass consumption with an affordable product, oftentimes adapted from a firm's already established commodity product, and to secure economies of scale and scope from relentless scaling.

Historically, this model worked well in the early stages when emerging markets were characterized as low cost, sourcing destinations and when local competition was insignificant. For example, after initial struggles in many Asian countries, Nike has found a formidable manufacturing

TABLE 3.1 *Conventional strategies and core assumptions*

Conventional entry strategy	Underlying core assumptions
Enter mass consumption markets, primarily commodities, in which unit costs can be scaled up through manufacturing and distribution	It is better to wait until markets consolidate as a result of common/similar demands than to nurture unfilled, but promising, market niches
Recalibrate existing products in order to reduce costs and to make them affordable	Affordable products are the most important factor; with commodities, consumers are already aware of the products and benefits for them
When appropriate, some features of the product and/or service can be localized to meet local needs and expectations	Localization is needed, but transferable marketing and manufacturing costs should not offset any cost advantage
Employ expats as experts and hire local talent	Expertise from the home country is generally preferred because the talent base in local markets tends to be limited
Construct supply chains that link the different manufacturing units to select markets	With proper scaling, it is imperative to link and integrate them through logistics and supply chain management

base in Vietnam. Most of these manufactured products were sourced to other countries as exports or as semifinished products. Although it was recognized that some local demands were manifest, these were minimal and inexpensive. However, unlike Nike or Coca-Cola, other storied firms, such as Wal-Mart, General Motors, Home Depot, Best Buy, and Nokia, have found that duplicating their success in emerging markets has not been as tractable.[3]

A variant of this strategy is to adopt this cost-based model (production centricity) with refinements for application in a marketing context (merchandising orientation). A representative example is a firm switching from building a large scale to reduce manufacturing costs to developing a mass consumption market for the sale of its products. In effect, the logic changes from manufacturing to marketing in order to capitalize on the purchasing power of new consumers. For example, in athletic footwear, this involves a transition from sourcing manufacturing to selling similar products for mass consumption. Conventional wisdom suggested that firms with dominant business models and superior resources, typically large and reputable MNCs, should leverage their advantages in emerging markets. This was to be facilitated by globalization and technological advances that had created a homogenous, global marketplace.[4]

All too often, however, it was assumed that consumer demand would be similar, and that local competition would be minimal. Hence, "localization" primarily meant refinements of the global product to accommodate nuanced local preferences. Significant transformations of the product were not fully expected, and the costs of accommodating these refinements were thought not to be substantial. As we discuss in the next section, several, if not all, of these assumptions did not apply to our study sample.

Reassessing conventional thinking

In our field interviews, there were indications that surging market segments, such as the middle class in emerging markets, possessed different consumption preferences, and that there were signs that these prevailing assumptions about mass marketing merchandising had changed (see Box 3.1). As argued in this report, the changes are particularly salient in the consumer goods and retailing industry sectors.

The experience of China's instant noodle stalwart, Kangshifu, is instructive in this regard.[5] At first, the company simply duplicated its business model that had worked so effectively in Taiwan, thinking that mainstream Chinese consumers would react in a similar fashion. Much to the company's dismay, however, the company was unsuccessful in attracting consumers to its fold, prompting the realization that previous business models did not comport well with a changed environment. Humbled, but undaunted, they then revised the strategy to cater to the local needs of the mainland that accounted for more demanding consumers. These changes involved using a new brand name that was appropriate to the Chinese style (Kangshifu), introducing a price point that was consistent with the consumption preferences of mainland consumers, and positioning their products at the mid-market. This adaptation proved to be very successful. Currently, Kangshifu is noted for its ability to differentiate itself from the mainland offerings of low-end instant noodles products.

A belief that is more widely accepted is that firms in emerging markets should accentuate the changing norms and preferences of local markets. To some degree, this belief was foreshadowed in certain celebrated business cases, such as Hindustan Unilever (HUL), which pioneered the use of sachet-packaging because their customers, unlike their counterparts in developed countries, could not afford products other than in small quantities. Currently, HUL sells 70% of its shampoo in one-use sachets for the equivalent of a couple of cents.[6] Similarly, Smart Technologies in the Philippines introduced a feature in cell phones in which people could recharge their phones with other cell phones using over-the-air technology.[7] Reflecting an understanding of the local market, in Malaysia, Maxwell House and Oreo have likewise changed their products to fit the local market and now enjoy the reputation of being the top two brands as evaluated by local consumers.[8]

As these examples demonstrate, the success of these firms did not occur by simply adopting a previous model that worked well in developed economies. Nor did success arise solely from a sheer transition from a manufacturing to a marketing logic. Success also did not ensue simply by adhering to a similar growth model. In most of these cases, success resulted from a radical transformation of an existing business model to accommodate deep-seated local needs. Yet, it is tempting to adapt features of a good model to a new market, particularly for firms that have strong global reputations. Localization has become more compelling with the development of emerging markets. Over a short period, there has been a transformation of local consumer expectations in emerging markets to which firms, both foreign and local, need to be more attentive.[9] We defer a full discussion of localization to later chapters in this book. To their credit, some of these MNCs have begun to refashion their strategies and recalibrate their product offerings accordingly. We will discuss some of these changes in the later part of this book.

BOX 3.1 *Asia's emerging middle class*

Among the surging market niches that have changed the competitive landscape is that of the middle class that has become more affluent in emerging markets. A belief that is becoming more widely recognized is that a vibrant and prosperous middle class is essential to the healthy functioning of modern capitalism. This belief is stridently advocated by Nobel laureate Joseph Stiglitz and former secretary of labor Robert Reich, who both view inequality and the resulting shrinking of the middle class as the core reason for today's economic stagnation.

In the context of emerging markets, however, the obverse of this— the rise of the middle class—is seen as significantly contributing to the sharp decline in world poverty. Official sources indicate that close to 680 million people were lifted out of poverty in China alone between 1981 and 2001. Similar rates of growth can describe India's ascendancy through poverty reduction, where between 200 and 300 million people have been lifted out of poverty. In all, the decline in extreme poverty comes from the growth and development of the middle-class sectors in emerging markets.

How large is this resurging middle-class sector in emerging markets? In a SEIMS (Skolkovo Institute for Emerging Market Studies) Issue report, economist William T. Wilson presents his projections and quantification of the middle class, which are excerpted here:

- "China has at least 400 million people on the threshold of becoming globally middle class. It will lead the world in adding people to these ranks over the next 15 years."
- "India will replace China as the biggest contributor to the global middle class around 2027."
- "Asia, currently home to 28% of the world's global middle class, is projected to account for two-thirds by 2030."
- "In terms of its impact on global economic growth, consumer spending between the emerging and developed market economies is now roughly equal."
- "While income inequality may be rising rapidly within most countries, the distribution of global income among countries is rapidly becoming more equal."

Even so, despite the growth and allure of the middle class, it remains to be seen how consumers in this sector will respond to current products and services. Specifically, consumers' tastes, preferences, needs, and aspirations need to be defined and closely monitored. The ability of firms to recognize these needs and to provide for appropriate products and services will ultimately lead to their relative success or failure in these sectors.

Sources: Adapted from http://www.economist.com/blogs/economist-explains/2013/06/economist-explains-0#sthash.f2n805MY.dpuf; William T. Wilson, *Hitting the Sweet Spot: The Growth of the Middle Class in Emerging Markets*. EY, EMEIA MAS 1455.0313 (2013); Joseph Stiglitz, *The Price of Inequality: How Today's Divided Society Endangers Our Future* (New York: W. W. Norton, 2012, 2013); Robert Reich, *Aftershock: The Next Economy and America's Future* (New York: Vintage Books, 2010, 2011).

Changes in inflection points

What precise elements of the conventional logic failed? The term "inflection point," originating in differential calculus, is generally defined as the point in which directionality (plus to minus and vice versa) or the basic form (convexity to concavity and vice versa) changes.[10] As applied to business and strategy, it is a fundamental change in core assumptions that alters the basis of competition. The term gained wider popularity when the then Intel chairman Andrew Grove spelled out changes in inflection points that triggered transformations in his company's core strategy.[11] Inflection points are also used synonymously with the terms "sea-change," "game change," "tipping point," and "disruptive change."

On the basis of extensive interviews with representatives from the leading consumer goods sector in Asia, along with an in-depth review of changes in emerging markets, we arrived at inflection points that describe the changing competitive contour of emerging markets, particularly in the context of consumer goods and retailing (Table 3.2). Fundamentally, they represent a shift from cost-driven to demand-enhancing competition. Instead of a fixation on mass consumption (commodity) markets, more attention is directed at an analysis of propitious market niches

TABLE 3.2 *Changes in inflection points*

Traditional model	Contemporary model
Manufacturing scale	Premium product scale
Guanxi-based	Competence-based
Cost	Quality, brand
Supply-oriented	Demand-oriented
Opportunity chasing	Competence-based
Growth-oriented	Profit-oriented
Overseas reliance	Local reliance
Product branding	Product category branding
Mass manufacturing	Category-based flexible manufacturing
Standardized channels	Differentiated channels
Expatriates/hiring local talent	Training local talent
Selling products	Serving customers
Commodity-based marketing	Niche-based (multiple "touch" points)
Following the government's order	Anticipating the government's action
KPI (Key Performance Indicators): profits; market share; cost efficiency	KPI (Key Performance Indicators): profitable growth over time; enhanced consumer benchmarks

using intensive consumer research.[12] They also signal pivotal changes in the manner in which competitive advantages are defined and developed, specifically the increased importance of competence-based learning instead of relying solely on relational capital.

These inflection points were described by interview-respondents in different contexts. Anthony Tsai (whom we introduced earlier) underscores the need for more research on the consumer. "There are unmet markets with a still evolving and undefined consumer. They tend not to be loyal to a brand," he said, "but nonetheless they are very price-conscious." However, while they are price-conscious, they also seek premium products with attractive branding (much like a preference for "the cheapest of high-end Rolex watches"). Despite their relative degree of newly found affluence, they are also still relatively insecure in their purchase decisions. Firms have to offer a variety of attractive cues to boost their purchases. Hence, they comprise the "multi-touch" consumer for which "good attention is warranted." To address this, Tsai recommends a "regimen of brand portfolios."

Earlier treatises about a fast-growing middle class incorporate some degree of insecurity, reflecting the tension between attaining a new level of recognized affluence and the fear that this newfound wealth might be temporary or short-lived. Hence, in China, for example, there is that constant effort to abide with what some sociologists call "conspicuous consumption," or what is defined as "an underlying impulse to demonstrate a person's belonging to a certain status group, a new moneyed elite, that is still unsure of its social boundaries and its relations with the rest of Chinese society."[13] Similarly, in an ethnographic study, Li Zhang notes:

> Their [Chinese] social insecurity is thus partially derived from their hyper-awareness of negative public perceptions. This sense of insecurity drives many of them to seek not only conspicuous material consumption but also excessive investments in cultivating their children's talents and abilities in order to prepare them to become cultured elites. Consumption thus becomes the main conduit to gain cultural and symbolic capital, and the key for claiming and authenticating social status.[14]

In context, multi-branding becomes the strategy to flank a wide range of purchasing options. Along with the emphasis on brand is the importance of knowing the consumer, because macroeconomic growth in developing countries has given rise to a new breed of middle-income consumers, but with different tastes and preferences than more stereotyped conceptions of similar affluent segments.

Collectively, these findings offer implications for new strategies in emerging markets. The transition from the traditional to the contemporary has not been continuous or seamless, but uneven and inconsistent, prompting some researchers to see paradoxes and inconsistencies in the consumer behavior of middle-class sectors.

A new model is needed, but what type of model?

Notes

1. William Wilson and Nikolay Ushakov, "Brave new world categorizing the emerging market economies—a new methodology," SKOLKOVO Emerging Market Index (February 2011).
2. S. Shankar, C. Ormiston, N. Bloch, R. Schaus, and V. Vishwanath, "How to win in emerging markets," *MIT Sloan Management Review,* Spring 2008. 49(3):18–24. The authors argue the entering mass markets act as a defense for multinationals against competitive homegrown local firms that have begun to enter higher premium niches. In addition, the authors argue for localization, local hires, a cost mentality, favorable acquisitions, and overall efficiency. Accordingly, while entry into mass markets still retains a production-centric modality, it can be considered to be more as an evolving strategy to meet the new requirements of emerging markets.
3. For a good reading on why firms fail in emerging markets and what can be done, see Tarun Khanna, Krishna Palepu, and Jayant Sinha, "Strategies that fit emerging markets," *Harvard Business Review,* June 2005, https://hbr.org/2005/06/strategies-that-fit-emerging-markets.
4. For a good exposition and critique, see K. E. Meyer and Y. T. Tran, "Market penetration and acquisition strategies for emerging markets," *Long Range Planning,* 2006. 39(2):177–197.
5. This narrative is based on the following sources: http://wwwfoods1.com/content/909174/; http://masterkomg.com.cn; and http://money.163.com 12/0619/00/84ASO53300253B0H.html.
6. See Maria Letelier, Fernando Flores, and Charles Spinosa, "Developing productive customers in emerging markets," *California Management Review,* Summer 2003. 45(4): 77–103.
7. Jamie Anderson and Costas Markides, "Strategic innovation at the base of the pyramid," *MIT Sloan Management Review,* Fall 2007. 49(1):83–88, and p. 84 in particular; also see Shankar et al., "How to Win in Emerging Markets," 18–24.
8. http://www.doc88.com/p-293361434347.html.
9. For a good assessment of successful and failed strategies, refer to Letelier, "Developing productive customers in emerging markets."

10 Eric W. Weisstein, "Inflection point." From *MathWorld*—A Wolfram Web Resource. http://mathworld.wolfram.com/InflectionPoint.html.
11 Andrew Grove, *Only the Paranoid Survive: How to Exploit the Crisis Point That Challenges Every Company* (New York: Random Books, 1999).
12 A good analysis of multi-branding in emerging markets is addressed by Amitava Chattopadhyay and Rajeev Batra, *The Emerging Market Multinationals* (New York: McGraw Hill, 2012). The authors build a case for four different types of brands, depending on product segments and industry maturation. They cover differentiation as well as cost advantages of different branding strategies. In this book, we focus on the former.
13 Attributed to Christopher Buckley, "How a Revolution Becomes a Dinner Party: Stratification, Mobility, and the New Rich in Urban China." In *Culture and Privilege in Capitalist Asia*. Michael Pinches, ed. (New York: Routledge, 1999). Cited by John Osburg, *Anxious Wealth: Money and Morality among China's New Rich* (Stanford: Stanford University Press, 2013), p. 127.
14 Li Zhang, *In Search of Paradise: Middle-Class Living in a Chinese Metropolis* (New York: Cornell University Press, 2010), p. 9.

4
New Logics-Scaling the Tail

Abstract: *The major premises of Chris Anderson's "long tail" theory are presented here with implications for emerging markets. Anderson's formulation is that, under specific conditions, value will not reside in the mean, but in the peripherals (or the tail). Hence, overall sales form peripherals or the "long tail" will outnumber sales from the mean of the distribution. As applied to emerging markets, value-creation reflects a shift from supply to demand considerations: entry in mass consumption markets is ceding ground to investments in smaller but propitious market segments, many of which were largely unfilled in the past. After a review of three types of scaling used in prior studies, we adopt a new type based on features of agglomeration for the clustering of multi-brand linkages—contiguous interconnections.*

Park, Seung Ho, Gerardo R. Ungson, and Andrew Cosgrove. *Scaling the Tail: Managing Profitable Growth in Emerging Markets.* New York: Palgrave Macmillan, 2015. DOI: 10.1057/9781137538598.0012.

In the bestseller, *The Long Tail*, analyst Chris Anderson spells out a new form of competition and value-creation.[1] His basic advocacy is premised on indelible changes that influence how demand and supply are linked and configured. In this chapter, we discuss the conception of value-creation with specific references to innovation with a particular life cycle of a product. From conventional concepts, we then introduce and amplify Anderson's basic theory to what we call "scaling the tail," which is the overarching theoretical anchor in our study.

From conventional to contemporary value-creation

In Figure 4.1, we describe a proposed progression in value-creation. The first figure (4.1a) depicts the traditional concept of value-creation. Known popularly as the normal or the Gaussian distribution, it emphasizes the pattern of sales, in which 90–95% of sales fall within an area relatively close to the mean, depending on their distance or standard deviation. In this case, the outliers generally fall within the tail or the marginal space, ranging from 5 to 10% (for this reason, statisticians generally test hypotheses based on assessments of cases that fall within one- or two-tail parameters). While not formulated in the precise context of value-creation, it has been used to describe the diffusion of innovation in marketing, as well as disruption patterns in technological adaptations.[2]

Among the first variations of the normal distribution is expanding the application and sale of a product through reconceptualized extensions. We refer to this as "straddling the curve" (Figure 4.1b).[3] Made famous by former McKinsey consultant and bestselling author Kenichi Ohmae, this depiction involves product extensions that ignite new market demands.[4] In Ohmae's conception, the variations out of the standard transistor radio manufactured by Sony Corp. gave rise to televisions, cameras, computers, and various peripherals. Perhaps the modern application can be gleaned by the array of new versions of Microsoft's Windows and other related operating systems. The advantage of product extensions is the familiarity of consumers with the basic brands, which reduces the costs of creating market demand for entirely new products. It is important to note, however, that straddling the curve still centers the application on the main product or brand, even if newer market segments arise from subsequent applications.

Anderson's new formulation of value-creation is depicted in Figure 4.1c. Its popularity in both practitioner and academic circles derives from its transformation of traditional conceptions: value resides not in the mean, but in the peripherals (or the tail). For example, sales in declining brick-and-mortar bookstores have shifted from popular books sold mainly in stores to the hard-to-obtain books that can be seamlessly ordered and delivered online. For Anderson, sales generated by the accumulation of books at the tail can outpace the volume from brick-and-mortar bookstores. Given the advances in information and storage technologies, the incremental cost of locating a previously hard-to-find book has become relatively low. In contrast, in a brick-and-mortar warehouse, suppliers will need to stack up every conceivable book to deliver a similar service—a physical impossibility.

As applied to emerging markets, there are a number of implications that can be derived from Anderson's work and from our earlier discussion of inflection points (Table 3.2). In Figure 4.1d, we introduce our conception of "scaling the tail." Consistent with new trends, value-creation follows a new pattern: a shift from supply to demand considerations, such that entry in mass consumption markets is ceding ground to investments in smaller but propitious market segments, many of which were largely unfilled in the past. Structurally, this model combines features from straddling the curve (Figure 4.1b) with the long tail (Figure 4.1c). In context, the center of gravity has shifted from mass consumption to specialized niches. Moreover, the selection and nurturing of choice brands (or power brands) now becomes a key ingredient for accommodating the requirements of these specialized niches. Although there

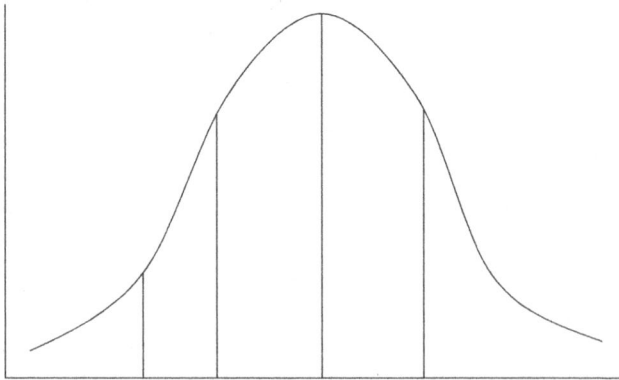

A *Conventional normal distribution*
Source: Everett Rogers, *Diffusion of Innovation*, 3rd ed. (New York: Free Press, 1963), p. 247.

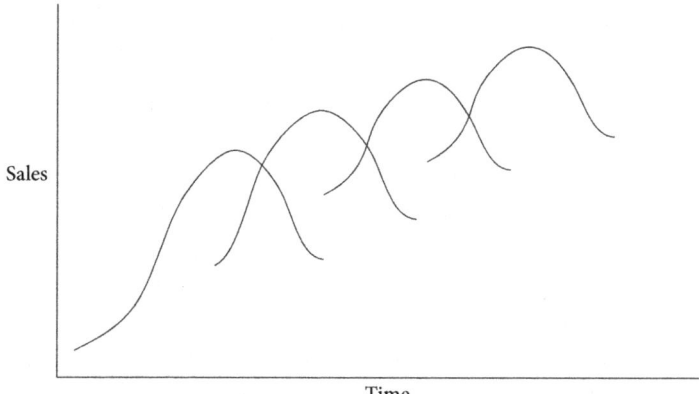

B *Straddling the "curve with incremental innovations"*

Through tweaks and product improvements, the sales-growth curve can be extended over time.

Source: Keniche Ohmae, *The Mind of the Strategist: The Art of Japanese Business* (New York: McGraw Hill, 1982). Adapted and extended from narrative on pp 151–152.

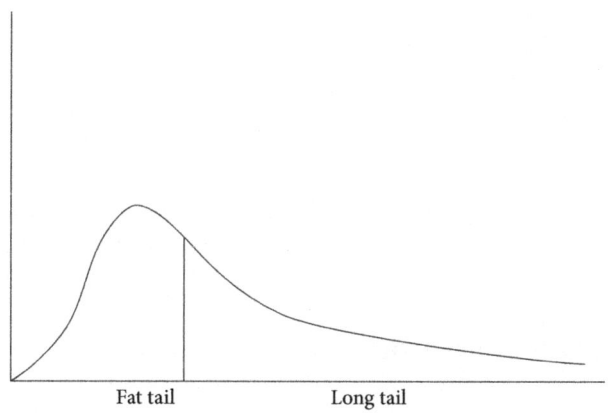

C *The long tail*

Note: In C. Anderson's depiction, sales from the "Long Tail" can eventually outpace growth in mainstream sales over time.

Source: Chris Anderson, *The Long Tail: Why the Future of Business Is Selling Less for More* (New York: Hyperion Books, 2006). Adapted from figures 1 and 2, pp 54–55.

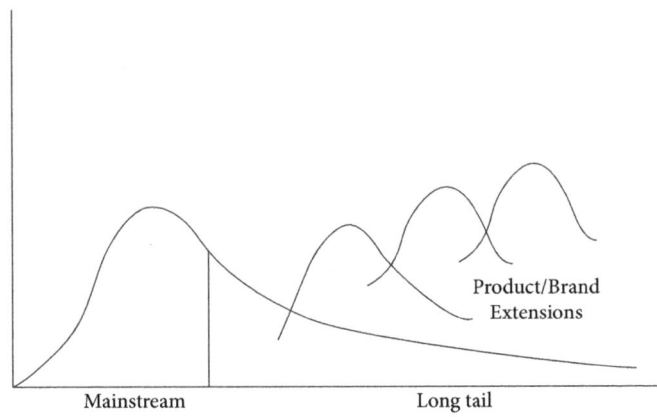

D Scaling the tail

Note: This reformulation proposes that sales from the long tail, far from being isolated but large in a cumulative sense, can be scaled with timely brand/product extensions. This is particularly manifest in pockets of middle-class affluence in emerging markets, such as China.

FIGURE 4.1 The progression of value-creation

are different types of previously unfilled market niches, the common one referred to by respondents in this context is the growing middle-class sector (see Box 4.1). But it is not enough to simply offer one or two brands, as might have been the practice in low-priced commodity products. Brand portfolio, in the words of Anthony Tsai, involves "flanking different segments" with well-positioned brands—a critical arsenal in this strategy. However, what does flanking in context mean?

Flanking and multi-branding

Recently, Jill Avery and Michael Norton, both researchers at the Harvard Business School, have implored marketing researchers to start exploring extreme customers, or those situated at the tail-ends of the distribution, for critical information.[5] Their advocacy comports well with our own focus on what occurs at the tail-ends and the extent to which firms in emerging markets need to be attentive to them. As indicated earlier, these tail-ends represent surging market segments that were previously dormant. Much like a resurgent volcano, however, these segments have created a new imperative that impels a different approach to servicing them.

In our interviews, respondents suggested flanking segments that entail the development of similarly related brands that are oriented to specific market segments. This main difference between scaling the tail and the long tail is precipitated by a new and emerging market sector (the middle class) with specialized needs. In Anderson's work, the hard-to-locate items that fall within the long tail, although voluminous, are also fragmented. However, he argues that over time, the aggregation of these items can outnumber the sales of popular items located in the center of the distribution. In this work, we depart from this original formulation in arguing that those high-end brands in the periphery can indeed be aggregated, but that they also can be effectively scaled.

Moreover, growth is no longer linear or continuous, but it is uneven and follows a "granular" pattern, in which certain pockets of opportunities, such as affluent Tier 1 (major markets or cities) and Tier 2 (secondary markets or cities) coexist alongside with standardized products in Tier 3 (minor markets or cities) and Tier 4 (peripheral markets or cities).[6] Granular analysis eschews growth based on averages, and favors clusters of concentrated growth based on consumers' preferences for product categories.[7] In all, a contingency logic applies to the types of consumer products. According to Anthony Tsai, the standard cost-drive model still works well in commodities, but in sectors such as health, fashion, food, beauty products, and detergents, differentiation has become the new mantra as the engine of growth.

Given the importance of selecting market segments and positioning brands, competency-based learning has become much more critical. Learning about consumer nuances within a market niche is oftentimes more difficult than obtaining general knowledge about a standard brand. Undoubtedly, relational capital or cultivating close connections as a form of knowledge is still important, but competency learning has become more critical. This is because the dynamics of multi-branding (additional brands that center on a specific product category) and granular growth (specific clusters of growth) create important differences in terms of how scaling can occur. In order to achieve effective learning in this regard, we distinguish between aggregation and contiguous interconnection and their concomitant effects on scaling in the next two sections (Table 4.1).

TABLE 4.1 *The long tail and scaling the tail: implications for emerging markets (EM)*

The long tail (Chris Anderson)	Scaling the tail (reapplied to EM)
A non normal distribution in which a disproportionate number of cases occurs far from its center	New value is created from sales in previously unfilled market niches than in the traditional concentrated commodity markets
Significant profits can accrue to large sales from the aggregation of rare items instead of the mass market	Significant profits are created from the agglomeration of a platform of different brands instead of one standard brand/product
Focus is less on tangible (brick-and-mortal retailing) as it is on more intangible (online, virtual) points of inventory storage and distribution	Focus is less on centralized retailing as it is on scaling high-end brands with similar consumer demand
Emphasis is on lowered incremental costs, as opposed to lower per unit costs	Emphasis is on covering the added costs of differentiation through select price points, as opposed to lower per unit costs
Pareto distribution does *not* apply to the "tail."*	Pareto distribution applies selectively, depending on the type of brand product and the selection of segments
Market mechanisms can be significantly altered by changes in inflection points (e-commerce)	Market mechanisms are defined by less restricted inflection points that are ingrained in deep consumer preferences and expectations

Note: * Anderson's treatment of power laws, specifically the Pareto Law, is more nuanced than simply stated here. He acknowledges that the 80/20 rule still holds, though not necessarily in the proportion that is commonly interpreted (Anderson, *The Long Tail*, pp. 134–135). Supporters and critics of Anderson differ on the actual proportion of the distribution, the placement demarcating the short and the long tail, and whether to use percentages or actual numbers to demarcate the boundaries. For specific references, see http://en.wikipedia.org/wiki/Long_tail.

Three types of scaling

To understand how scaling can occur in the periphery of the tail, we further differentiate between three types of scaling. The conventional interpretation of scaling is operating at a higher volume of production or sales with much lower unit costs ("scaling out"). In other words, operating plant capacity with 100,000 units can be done more efficiently than one with 100 units. A second type of scaling is franchising or morphic replication, such as in the case of McDonalds or Starbucks, that expands in ways that efficiently capture its standardized features. In this case, the term "scaling across" is used. A third type of scaling is expansion through interconnectedness, in which there is a deeper penetration across a specific product category (also termed "scaling in"). Some typical examples include Honda's use of a common engine for its different products, or P & G's flanking of different brands for detergents.[8] In this case, there is a strategic focus on a specific company as a general proxy for different brands, such as Nike in athletic footwear, across different spatial/geographic territories.

The concept of contiguous interconnection is based on agglomeration that has been historically described to explain the dynamics of contiguous or spatial concentration in geographical space, such as in cities or specialized zones (see Box 4.1).[9] The economics of agglomeration emphasize interlinkages and increasing returns that arise from precipitating factors. For example, in the case of California's Silicon Valley, the confluence of venture capital, a supportive entrepreneurial climate, the spillover from leading-edge universities, and a favored access for highly talented immigrants have led to a spatial concentration that is distinctive and enduring. In this study, we adopt features of agglomeration, but situate the clustering in the context of multi-brand linkages, which we call *contiguous interconnections* (Box 4.1).

BOX 4.1 *Contiguous interconnections—agglomeration as applied to this study*

Our adaptation of contiguous interconnectedness is based largely on agglomeration dynamics. Agglomeration generally refers to the clustering of activities based on locality. The study of agglomeration has had a rich history dating back as far as Max Weber, Alfred Marshall, and has recently been extended to the study of economic growth, urban concentration, special economic zones, technology center and clusters, and related applications. Hence, agglomeration intersects multiple academic disciplines including economics, urban studies, sociology, geography, chemistry, and food studies.

While there are multiple variants and conceptualizations of agglomeration at the present time, we posit a particular extension— *contiguous interconnections*—for which a number of shared attributes constitute its basic understanding:

- *Clustering*—the gathering together and union of different parts or items into a meaningful construct;

- *Locality*—the centrality of a specific location that defines and inhabits the collected mass;
- *Spatial modality*—the physical and virtual space of place, time, and category that constitutes locality and clustering;
- *Network effects*—pooling and common access to resources give rise to increasing returns to scale;
- *Spillovers*—benefits are subject to economies of scale and scope, increasing the size of any installed base;
- *Interlinked nodes*—nodes or pivot points of carrying capacity in a network are connected systemically;
- *Learning*—increased know-how is enhanced through a process of "cumulative causation," in which cause-and-effect are interlinked and systemically developed over time.

In our adaptation of contiguous interconnections to scaling the tail, three qualifications are advanced. First, such interconnections can be further distinguished from aggregation. In treatises about value-creation using statistical distribution, sales at the tail tend to be voluminous in total, but fragmented and episodic in character. Think of the sale of a rare book, a musical score, or an old film. Taken in aggregate, these can comprise a large volume at the tail, but sales remain fragmented. In our study, agglomeration makes more sense than aggregation. Second, the introduction of multiple brands is aimed at creating some network effects; each brand builds on the other as the desired position in a targeted consumer mindset. Hence, in addition to physical and spatial proximity, there are likewise cognitive associations and linkages that go beyond traditional conceptions of agglomeration. Third, locality, in this sense, is represented by a common pool of consumers—the rising middle class that is more affluent and possesses a different set of consumption preferences. Although the middle class tends to be fragmented in terms of not necessarily sharing a common space, they are similar in terms of their income category and their responsiveness to particular price/product cues. Following the logic of the McKinsey Study, the middle class is also bounded together in terms of geographies, or clustering within major (Tier 1) and secondary (Tier 2) cities. Furthermore, their preferences are most pronounced in shopping decisions in malls and stores.

Sources: Masahisa Fujita and Jacques-Francois Thisse, *Economics of Agglomeration, Industrial Location, and Regional Growth* (New York: Cambridge University Press, 2002); Zoltán J. Ács and Attila Varga, "Entrepreneurship, Agglomeration and Technological Change." *Small Business Economics*, 1992. 24(2):115–138; and Nicholas A. Phelps, "External Economies, Agglomeration and Flexible Accumulation." *Transactions of the Institute of British Geographers, New Series*, 1992. 17(1): 35–46. Published by the Royal Geographical Society (with the Institute of British Geographers). URL: http://www.jstor.org/stable/622635. Mehrdad Baghai, Sven Smit, and S. Patrick Viguerie. McKinsey Solutions Report, Granular Growth: Granular Growth is a unique approach to assessing growth performance and developing robust growth strategies. http://solutions.mckinsey.com/granulargrowth.

In our study, contiguous interconnection is prevalent, in that synergy is created and enhanced from spatial linkages, or the close proximity of products or brands that are focused on a specific sector.[10] In network theory and computer architecture, expanding capacity is a matter of creating more nodes (pockets of information) or more processing functions within a node.[11] By expanding the number of nodes, the carrying capacity is increased. Such is reflected in a scaling out process. However, processing functions within a single node can likewise create linkages. Such is the case in a scaling-in process. If similar structural architectures are increased, without any change in the number of nodes or processing functions within a node, this is akin to the replicative type of scaling.

Contiguous interconnection occurs when pools of similar product spaces and extensions, notably in high-end brand segments, can be effectively enlarged through scaling. Marketers typically use multidimensional scaling and conjoint analysis to assess the perceptions of proximity within products.[12] The full benefits of contiguous interconnection materialize only when there is interdependence in perception, such that the perception of one brand is enhanced by the appreciation of another. Contiguous interconnection is also linked to network effects. For example, a cell phone might not work effectively with just one radio tower, but when pools of proximate towers are used, signals are enhanced and effective transmission is achieved.[13] These differences in scaling and their effects are summarized in Table 4.2.

TABLE 4.2 Scales, definitions, examples, and implications

Type of scale	Definition	Examples	Implications
Scale-up	Expansion to larger volumes or operating capacity is generally accompanied by lower unit costs	Plant size increases	Growth is linear; economies of scale and scope are prevalent
Scale-across	Expansion is through the replication of the standard business model across regions and markets	Franchises (McDonald, Starbucks)	Growth is reproductive; transferable marketing and manufacturing costs have to be significantly less; standardization is the norm
Scale-in	Expansion is through deeper penetration of a set of products or brands	Product brand flanking (Procter & Gamble)	Growth is granular; contiguous interconnection effects occur when consumers identify a set of similar and related products in a clear product space

Our adaptation of the phrase "scaling the tail" is less about scaling out (larger plant size) or scaling across (replicating McDonald outlets, for example), as it is more on deeper brand penetration, or scaling in (consolidating a product space of an acknowledged leader). This is enabled by consumer acceptance of the company's leadership in a product space (e.g., Rolex is considered to be a high-end brand, which is advantageous as it extends its brand across its different products).

New imperatives

To address changing consumer tastes across a particular product space, a plethora or platform of brands is created, not just a single brand, by new product brands or added product extensions. Examples include P & G's portfolio of brand detergents, which include BOLD Antikal, TIDE Fairy, DASH Flash, and others. Nestle's cereal brands include Cookie Crisp, Crunch, Finesse, Forced Flakes, and others.[14] Kraft Malaysia SdnBhd offers a broad product portfolio encompassing five consumer sectors: biscuits, confectionery, beverages, cheese, and grocery, in which each category enjoys a strong and distinctive image.[15]

Assessing the range of targeted consumer segments is attained through deep consumer behavior research. Balanced implementation can involve advertising the company as opposed to a single brand, such as Nike or GE, as symbols of reputable brands, for example, or in some selected categories, such as a localized product. Want Want China Holdings Limited's success as a sales-snack food covers an array of products, such as Rice Crackers, Gummies and Soft Chew Candies, Wafer Rolls and Puff Pastries, Ball Cake, Coated Nuts, Ice Popsicles, as well as biscuits, ice pops, candy, roasted seeds and nuts, baby melts, puffs, and jellies.[16]

Though broad and differentiated product brands and extensions are necessary, they are neither new nor sufficient requirements for "scaling the tail." After all, the strategy has been successfully employed by Procter & Gamble, Unilever, Nestle, Cadbury, and other industry stalwarts in developed markets for decades. In marketing, the use of multi-brands increases the likelihood of more shelf space and for flanking around the major brand, but it can also be expensive and dissipate a firm's resources.[17] The novelty of the application in emerging markets in this study reflects the growing affluence of particularly new consumer segments, which has been described as the "new middle class" by industry analysts.[18]

Even so, it was noted that consumer behavior in these middle classes is different from their counterparts in developed economies. Respondents invoked the need to deeply examine the new "multi-touch, engaged consumer," who is not as "secure" or "confident" about purchase decisions. In this context, multi-brands are not used for reasons depicted in traditional marketing that have been described earlier, but for providing a variety of choices for the "insecure" consumer. Oftentimes, it takes a deep commitment to the local consumer base to meet their requirements.

In all, "scaling the tail" is based on the following requirements: a deep understanding of the consumers' expectations, preferences, nuances, and requirements; an assessment of how these brands resonate with targeted consumer segments across different industry segments, product groups, and geographical territories; and a balanced implementation of standardized messages and tempered localization as strategies to create a common consumer experience. Not surprisingly, there was considerable reference to localization and execution as the next logical steps in a comprehensive strategy to meet the full requirements of growth and development.

In order to identify and appraise these requirements, we designed a diagnostic framework aimed at differentiating between levels of performance of companies in this industry sector. While scaling the tail is understood principally in terms of market positioning, our interest reverted to how this condition can be related specifically to the requirements of broad differentiation, which is the underlying strategy in most consumer goods and retailing sectors, and attendant drivers and systems to support it. Additional insights about "scaling the tail" can be obtained using this framework.

Notes

1. Chris Anderson, *The Long Tail: Why the Future of Business Is Selling Less for More*.
2. Everett Rogers, *Diffusion of Innovation* (3d ed.) (New York: Free Press, 1963); Geoffrey A. Moore, *Crossing the Chasm* (New York: HarperCollins, 2002).
3. Our usage adopts what is commonly referred to in finance as the "long/short straddle," in which purchases of the same option have the same strike price and other related characteristics. Taken in our context, "straddling" refers to extensions of a specific product that add or create value for the category.
4. Keniche Ohmae, *The Mind of the Strategist: The Art of Japanese Business* (New York: McGraw Hill, 1982).
5. Jill Avery and Michael Norton, "Learning from extreme customers," *Harvard Business Review* (January 6, 2014).
6. McKinsey Solutions Report, *Granular Growth: Granular Growth Is a Unique Approach to Assessing Growth Performance and Developing Robust Growth Strategies.* http://solutions.mckinsey.com/granulargrowth.
7. Ibid.
8. For a good discussion of brand extensions and positioning, see Roger J. Best, *Market-Based Management: Strategies for Growing Consumer Value and Profitability* (Upper Saddle River, NJ: Prentice Hall, 1999).
9. See Nicolas A. Phelps, "External economies, agglomeration and flexible accumulation," *Transactions of the Institute of British Geographers, New Series*, 1992. 17 (1):35–46. Published by the Royal Geographical Society (with the Institute of British Geographers): http://www.jstor.org/stable/622635; and Zoltán J. Ács and Attila Varga, "Entrepreneurship, agglomeration and technological change," *Small Business Economics*, April 2005. 24(3), Special Issue on: "Causes and effects of new business creation; empirical evidence from the Global Entrepreneurship Monitor (GEM): 323–334. Published by Springer: http://www.jstor.org/stable/40229426.

10 The concept originated in the study of linkages and positive externalities arising from location and proximity. See Masahisa Fujita and Jacques-Francois Thisse, *Economics of Agglomeration, Industrial Location, and Regional Growth* (New York: Cambridge University Press, 2002). We have adopted this phenomenon in this study as relating to positive externalities arising from the interdependence and synergy among related brands, as perceived by a large segment of consumers.
11 See Scalability. Wikipedia, http://en.wikipedia.org/wiki/Scalability.
12 I. Borg and P. Groenen, *Modern Multidimensional Scaling: Theory and Applications* (2d ed.) (New York: Springer-Verlag, 2005), pp. 207–212.
13 "Fixing the Future," PBS Documentary, 2012.
14 http://www.pg.com/en_US/brands/index.shtml.
15 http://www.bloomberg.com/research/stocks/private/snapshot.asp?privcapId=33876198.
16 http://www.jxfqs.com/Item/Show.asp?m=112&d=50.
17 Philip Kotler, Swee Hoon Ang, Siew Meng Leong, and Chin Tiong Tan, *Marketing Management: An Asian Perspective* (Singapore: Prentice Hall, 1996), pp. 483–484.
18 EY (with William T. Wilson), "Middle class growth in emerging markets: Hitting the sweet spot," 2012, http://www.ey.com/GL/en/Issues/Driving-growth/Middle-class-growth-in-emerging-markets.

Part III
The "P-E-C" Framework

5
The Diagnostic "P-E-C" Framework

Abstract: *A synthetic integration can be realized through a systematic and sequential process that we call the P-E-C Framework. Specifically, it involves P or the positioning of a firm for sustained growth; E or the exploration of relevant drivers for growth; and C or the co-alignment of management systems to appropriate growth strategies. Positioning involves decisions relating to achieving competitive advantages through cost leadership or differentiation, with attention to specialized but unserved niches. The exploration of drivers relates to the question: How to build advantages from either of these strategies? Finally, co-alignment refers to the consistency between strategies and management systems. This framework guides our inquiry and field survey for the study. Details of the survey, specifically differences between higher and lower performing firms, are presented.*

Park, Seung Ho, Gerardo R. Ungson, and Andrew Cosgrove. *Scaling the Tail: Managing Profitable Growth in Emerging Markets.* New York: Palgrave Macmillan, 2015. DOI: 10.1057/9781137538598.0014.

Scaling the tail impels a different mindset, a new approach to strategy, and a recognition of differences between niche marketing and mass merchandising. In our assessment, a new strategic template based on more incisive interpretations of scaling might be appropriate for the new competitive landscape of emerging markets. By way of comparison, two recent books have addressed these changes in emerging markets. The first is Ruchir Sharma's *Breakout Nations: In Pursuit of the Next Economic Miracles*.[1] This provocative work explores promising resurgent nations and offers a sharp critique of the BRIC countries. Sharma's focus on the nation as his unit of analysis differs from our study of successful firms at the micro-level. The second book, by Amitava Chattopadhyay and Rajeev Batra, *The Emerging Market Multinationals*,[2] builds a case for four different types of brands, depending on product segments and industry maturation. Based heavily on field interviews, the book covers differentiation, as well as cost advantages, of different branding strategies. In our study, we focused primarily on the former by providing a theoretical underpinning supported by both field interviews and cross-sectional survey analysis.

The "P-E-C" framework

To achieve profitable growth, all of the different elements of the preceding analysis have to come together. This synthetic integration can be realized through a systematic and sequential process that we call the P-E-C Framework. Specifically, it involves **P** or the **positioning** of a firm for sustained growth; E or the exploration of relevant drivers for growth; and C or the **co-alignment** of management systems to appropriate growth strategies. The framework also guides our inquiry and methodology for the proposed study and is explained in detail in the next section.

P—Positioning for growth

In this section, we attempt to understand the path of development in terms of the choice between growth and profitability. Having staked out a position on profitability and market growth, the next question is: How do firms build advantages from either of these strategies? Depending on whether cost or differentiation advantages are targeted, answers to these questions will vary. It is important to know that cost advantages are generally derived from cost reduction, while differentiation derives from meeting consumers' needs. To the extent that a firm can lower costs significantly and price its product lower than its competitors, cost leadership is established. This generally assumes that products are similar, which is the case in a commodity product. The logic of differentiation is locating a unique, non-price attribute that is desired by a consumer group that is willing to pay a premium.

E—Exploring drivers for growth

Earlier, we examined different drivers of growth and performance. A good point of departure is in understanding the business model of the firm. In essence, a business model provides answers to the following questions: (1) Who is your customer?; (2) What does the customer value?; (3) What drives growth in this segment?; and (4) What is the firm's value proposition?

Profitable growth typically assumes the extension of the basic product either through scale or scope, in which case economies are achieved. Growth can also ensue through careful acquisitions and diversification. It embeds the notion of market dominance, which assures that a firm has lower variable costs compared to competitors, leading to both high profits and high market share. A good way to grow is usually by replicating a firm's business model in a new context. Therefore, to understand how to achieve profitable growth, we need to understand the underlying business model of firms that do achieve profitable growth.

The overarching question to be answered is: Given a firm's current situation, how should it achieve profitable growth? A firm may have already embarked on the path of high growth or high profit; then, how should they turn their high growth or high profit into profitable growth? What are the strategic options they could choose from and how should they select the optimal choice?

C—Co-aligning management systems with growth strategies

In this third part, the focus is on determining what type of management system is most appropriate and supportive of a particular growth strategy. A good business model in itself is not a guarantee of profitable growth. These strategies can lead to profitable growth only if they are executed well. This is especially important for firms in emerging markets because they generally lack management capabilities.[3] Good execution includes many aspects, such as leadership, organization structure, and incentive system. These elements may be different for firms from emerging markets.

Our approach in finalizing this phase is through the logic of contingency, that is, different types of systems that are appropriate for different growth strategies. There is no universal system that applies to all, although some elements of good management are shared. Even so, it is critical that the right management systems support a given growth strategy.

BOX 5.1 *The P-E-C framework for achieving profitable growth-summary*

The P-E-C Framework encompasses three stages of development that also guide our inquiry and methodology. From our initial study and review of the research literature, we find that these stages comprise sequential elements for achieving profitable growth:

P—Positioning. *Basic Question*: How does a firm position itself to gain a competitive advantage in cost, differentiation, focus, or some combination thereof?

E—Exploring growth drivers. *Basic Question*: What is the firm's operational platform? What are the specific drivers to achieve these advantages?

C—Co-alignment with management systems: *Basic Question*: How does a firm develop supportive structures, processes, and cultures to realize these advantages over time?

In essence, the use of the P-E-C Framework is both diagnostic in revealing gaps and problem areas and prescriptive in identifying processes to close the gaps and redress problem areas. Specifically, the Framework is helpful for firms that seek to define institutional voids and the lack of market mechanisms that are more endemic to emerging markets.

Phase II of the study—interviews and survey

The empirical portion of this study comprises three basic procedures: (1) analysis of all multinational companies operating in the region based on the secondary data sources; (2) in-depth interviews with select firms and an intensive review of the literature and related cases; and (3) field survey of a cross-section of multinational corporations (MNCs). The goals are complementary: the first elicits the benchmark for sustained high performance (i.e., sustained profitable growth) and the list of potential target companies for field studies; the second provides some fine-grained insights based on an inductive process to arrive at workable propositions; the third attempts to confirm or disconfirm these propositions and to identify specific drivers of the profitable growth strategy through a deductive process.

Our cross-sectional data analysis spanned several sectors of the consumer goods and retailing industry: (1) food (42%); (2) beverage (8%); (3) home and personal care (13%); (4) tobacco (5%); (5) apparel (6%); and (7) grocery retail (25%). A preliminary analysis of 94,743 firms (Appendix IV) covering these seven industries was conducted to determine their profit potential across the ten countries that were surveyed.[4] In addition, we examined differences between local and foreign multinationals and a smaller group of highly successful firms (those exhibiting profitable growth). The five-year average growth for local companies was 20.76%, with an average return on assets of 6.41%. Foreign multinationals fared slightly lower, with an average growth rate of 18.26% and with a higher return on assets of 7.92%. However, the exemplary group (profitable growth) had an average growth rate of 37.04% and return on assets of 18.39%. This range in performance provided the basis for examining finely grained differences between higher and lower performing firms.

We disaggregated the sample (n=253) into four quadrants of varying performance levels: (1) high profits, high growth (n=133); (2) high profits, low growth (n=29); (3) low profits, high growth (n=28); and (4) low profits, low growth (n=63). The intent was to examine fine-grained differences between these quadrants. In addition, the sample was subjected to different combinations of varying profit and growth. As a variant of sensitivity analysis, we examined for significant differences in means and modalities across different combinations and selected consistent findings across all these profitability levels. To this end, we found that the hybrid segments, that is, high profits, low growth and low profits, high growth, were aligned with higher and lower performance in terms of the patterns and direction of profits and sales growth. Hence, we confined our analysis to the extreme segments (high profits, high growth; low profits, low growth).

On the basis of these analyzes, the project team constructed detailed case studies of selected firms that were classified as profitable growth. In some of these cases, we were able to interview key managers. Altogether, the field study included interviews with over 30 thought leaders and Asia business unit leaders of global consumer products and retailing companies. Appendix I includes some of the names of those who participated in the study while leaving out the rest at their requests, whose names are also left anonymous in following chapters;[5] 276 C-suite and senior executives also participated in the study survey conducted by Economic Intelligence Unit on behalf of the project team.

To be clear, low performance does *not* mean poor performance, but rather performance that is relatively low when compared to others. Thus, in the ensuing analysis, the attributions are labeled "higher performing" and "lower performing," respectively. Moreover, the study confined itself to high performers, in view of the focus on profitable growth. In context, most of those firms in the consumer goods and retailing sector in Asia's emerging markets were identified as pursuing a differentiation strategy, nuanced on occasion by their pursuit of selected market niches and segments. Additional considerations that guided our methods for demarcating performance levels are based on a study of performance in the consumer and retailing sectors in Asia (Appendix IV).

Notes

1 Ruchir Sharma, *Breakout Nations: In Pursuit of the Next Economic Miracles* (New York: W. W. Norton, 2012).
2 Amitava Chattopadhyay and Rajeev Batra, *The Emerging Market Multinationals* (New York: McGraw Hill, 2012).
3 See Tarun Khanna and Krishna Palepu, *Winning in Emergent Markets: A Roadmap for Strategy and Execution* (Boston, MA: Harvard Business School Publishing, 2010).
4 The primary data sources include CMIE, ORBIS, the Database of Industrial Firms of China, and China Statistical Yearbook.
5 Contact the authors for details on the companies and interviewees who are left anonymous throughout the study.

6
Positioning Firms for Profitable Growth

Abstract: *Multinational corporations in emerging and developing markets are occasionally blindsided by nascent changes in the environment that they fail to recognize. If such changes are identified, unsuccessful firms tend to simply ignore or underestimate them. In doing so, positioning strategies can be seriously compromised and can lead to ineffective strategies and poor performance. On the basis of survey results, we report that higher performing firms can be differentiated from lower performing firms in terms of the following positioning elements: (1) a focus on balanced, not unqualified growth; (2) assessment of environmental volatility for granular growth; (3) resolution of contradictions; (4) securing data analytics and financial sources for investment; (5) attachment of high priority to emerging markets; and (6) a systematic mode of expansion.*

Park, Seung Ho, Gerardo R. Ungson, and Andrew Cosgrove. *Scaling the Tail: Managing Profitable Growth in Emerging Markets*. New York: Palgrave Macmillan, 2015. DOI: 10.1057/9781137538598.0015.

What differentiates firms that are able to achieve profitable growth over time from those that are not? What are the requirements for success? What can be said about transitional firms, or those that have not, as yet, reached profitable growth, but are at the threshold of doing so? What specific contexts underlie "scaling the tail"?

In the P-E-C Framework, positioning is the initial posture taken by firms to respond to, or anticipate changes in, the external environment. It describes how firms assess the trends and volatility of their external environments. The premise is that perceptions, whether these are correct or misplaced, have a palpable influence on strategic choices. A correct reading of the external environment facilitates proper positioning; an incorrect reading, defined as significantly different from the average firm, can lead to wrong strategic choices.

Positioning is generally conceptualized in broad macrostrategic terms. For example, in Porter's classic, *Competitive Strategy*, he views alignment in terms of generic strategies, which are classified in terms of cost/differentiation and the focus/scope of product-market activities. Accordingly, firms can develop a defensible competitive position by either (1) becoming a cost leader in broad or niche markets (a cost strategy), or (2) offering a feature that is valuable and what a potential buyer will pay for in broad or niche markets (a differentiation strategy).[1] Similarly, in the marketing literature, positioning refers to the centrality of a product or a brand in the mind of a consumer that should correspond to a firm's value proposition.[2]

After extensive meetings with EY, however, the IEMS research team decided that more fine-grained, micro-level positioning choices were more relevant to the consumer goods and retail sectors. From our initial interviews, the IEMS team found that most firms had been pursuing a differentiation strategy, defined in general as identifying and incorporating product attributes, which consumers as a whole value, independent of price, and for which they are willing to pay. This strategy is not altogether surprising in that they operate in a consumer sector in which branding constitutes a core strategy. While there are elements of cost reduction, the IEMS research team decided to examine these in the next section (drivers of performance) instead of positing cost leadership in itself as a principal choice of firms in this sector, for which there was very minimal variance.

Positioning Firms for Profitable Growth   53

In the field interviews, respondents emphasized how the consumer goods and retail environment had been changing in fundamental ways (i.e., changing inflection points). As indicated, the overarching challenge is relating these changes to new strategies to ensure that information, management processes, and incentives are properly executed in support of brand management. Along with brand penetration and extensions, interviewees discussed additional areas of strategic positioning needed to build capabilities. With this cumulative information, we next discuss how profitable growth firms position themselves for high performance.

Focus on balanced, not on unqualified, growth

The choice of key performance indicators underlies a firm's primary strategy. When properly designed, performance indicators operate as signals or beacons for strategic alignment, in addition to controls and validation of a firm's decisions and activities. Resource and personnel decisions are presumably made in accordance with a firm's primary strategy, as measured and monitored by performance indicators. What then are the key differences between higher and lower performing firms?

As indicated earlier, the pursuit of unqualified growth can be ill-fated. Growth is good, but to pursue growth that is not qualified by resources, strategic intent, and defensible opportunities can lead to unintended consequences. Hence, the consideration of major goals and objectives, termed KPI (Key Performance Indicators), is a part of strategic positioning. In our survey, firms with varying levels of performance differ in their perceptions of their most important KPI for the current year and for the next three years. High performing firms emphasize *operating profits* and see *market share growth* occurring in three years. In contrast, lower performing firms stress *growth in market share* and anticipate profits in the future. Consistent with earlier findings, however, securing profits in later years is not a guarantee unless scaling is achieved. In light of the difficulties in scaling, as presented earlier, it is not altogether surprising that the higher performers in the sample are able to secure profits first before pursuing growth (Figure 6.1).

Even so, this does not necessarily mean that short-term thinking (profits) is preferred to long-term (growth) results. In fact, in field interviews, respondents expressed different approaches to achieving profitable growth, to the extent that firms should emphasize profitability or growth. The chief customer officer of a global personal care firm suggests a combination of the two: "We don't compromise on the short term for the long term, and our CEO is very tough and talks to me about it a lot, very tough on delivering profitability all the time in all markets." Others assail the limitations of short-term thinking. One interviewee observes: "Too many companies come in with a European or American model which is very short term, but with emerging markets you need long-term thinking in order to build relationships." He adds: "This focus on profit and cost is a mono-focused one. It is a matter of getting the right balance."

How then might we reconcile these points of view along with survey results and empirics? With further analysis, we noted differences between multinational firms from developed countries (mostly from the United States, Europe, and Japan) and newly multinationals (competitive firms from parts of Asia). For the former, the focus on profits or growth depends on their corporate objectives. In the case of multinationals that have long operated in emerging markets, growth over profits is preferred. For other firms seeking to raise capital for local investment, the emphasis might be on profits.

We noted that the focus on profitability on the latter firms does not translate to traditional conceptions of short-term thinking, not at least in the manner understood in the developed world. As a point of comparison, consider the relatively high savings rates in developing countries when compared to those in developed economies. People save in this context because safety nets that might be taken for granted in developed economies are not present nor are they operative in institutionally devoid countries.

Similarly, for firms operating in emerging markets that seek capital from operations, they face capital and equity markets that are not as developed or as effective as those in the developed world. In such a case, firms might place a higher emphasis on profits. Considered in context, the attention on profitability might be short-term, but not without a significant consideration of significant long-term consequences. Without revenues to reinvest back into the business, long-term sustainability is not feasible. There is another reason that relates to granular growth and uneven economic development in regional markets—a point that is developed in the next section.

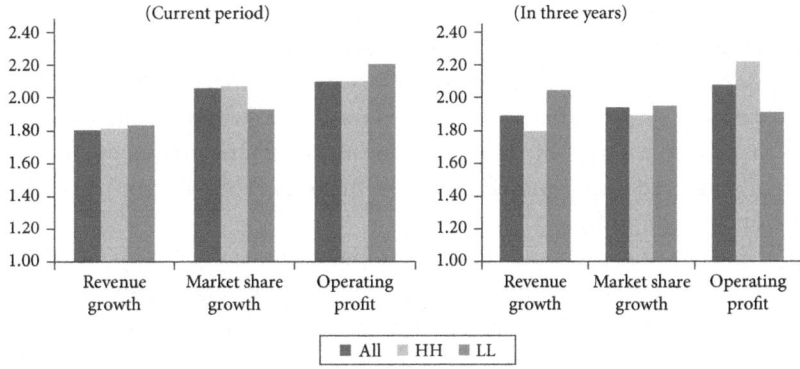

FIGURE 6.1 *Strategic objectives (current vs. in three years)*

Assess environmental volatility in terms of granular growth

A central feature in strategic management is the importance of a firm's perception of its external environment, specifically the extent to which the firm conceives of important shifts and changes, as a prelude to how the firm can respond to opportunities and threats. Historically, SWOT (strengths-weaknesses-opportunities-threats) analysis, along with modern variants, has been formulated based on subjective evaluations. In most treatises, the environment is treated in monolithic terms, or as in one major type of environment, typically the core industry sector, faced by the reference firm.

Our interviews indicate otherwise. As discussed previously, firms in emerging markets have to deal with granular growth. They have to address and service uneven pockets of economic development as potential markets. Geographical differences and infrastructure constitute important factors in the growth equation. As Godfrey Nthunzi, chief financial officer for Colgate Palmolive India, asserts; "The biggest challenge that we have in growing profitably in India is how to serve our diverse consumers who are geographically dispersed in a profitable manner. So, how to get our product to the consumer in a manner that actually makes business sense." He adds: "there is a focus of authorities [in India] on developing infrastructure to access parts of the country that previously would have been completely inaccessible and that population is giving us the opportunities that we see for further growth."[3]

To add further context to the above, other respondents talked about granularity in terms of a "multi-speed" world, one that is paced to standard products and the other to fast growth market segments. One interviewee suggests that "Companies need to take a portfolio approach to managing a range of different markets, different phases of development, being adaptive enough in those markets to move around, change the operating model as they go."

The CEO of a consumer goods company opines: "the way we look at growth is in a more granular manner ... a more advanced business model, compared to an entry into a country, we would go into more granularity in certain geographies where we may be underrepresented, certain trade channels where we can improve. So, we go in to a more granular level of looking for growth opportunities."

In order to accommodate this imperative, companies need to be very attentive to market changes and environmental volatility. In our survey, higher performing firms are more aware of the changes arising from demand volatility, competition, local market regulation, pressure from HQ, and changes in consumer behaviors when compared to lower performing firms. As indicated, perceptions are important to the extent that they are also consequential. Unless changes are perceived, no actions will ensue. In similar manner, if changes are misconstrued, then the wrong action will occur. Greater awareness generally leads to better anticipation of changes in a firm's strategy (Figure 6.2).

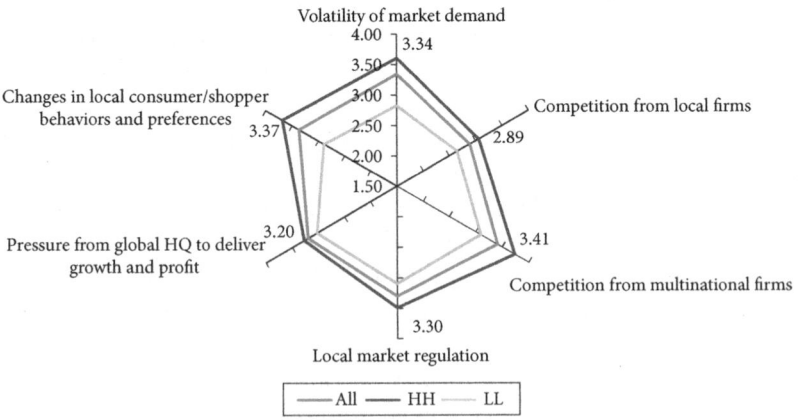

FIGURE 6.2 *External drivers of firm strategy*

Similarly, perceptions of market share changes influence a firm's strategy and future positioning. In our context, such perceptions can have a significant impact on a firm's confidence in its abilities to sustain its strategy. Anticipating future market growth can bolster a strategy for further investment, while lower expectations can result in a more cautious bearish strategy. Informed perceptions are based on good and reliable data. The consumer goods CEO of an Indonesian unit argues: "You have to have the data to understand what social and economic standards people have in different geographies; you need to understand the adjacent businesses... when people come from Java, they come with a certain preference in what they like to consume. So, you need to have that information."

In the survey, higher performing firms anticipate increases in market share over time; in contrast, lower performing firms are more pessimistic about improving their performance. This finding is consistent with a firm's confidence in its basic strategy to pursue future growth (Figure 6.3).

Resolve contradictions in emerging markets

In the midst of change, it is to be expected that business models emerge that reflect the transition from one state of affairs to another. The trajectory toward scaling the tail reflects such a transition. As such, profitable growth in emerging Asia impels consumer products and retail

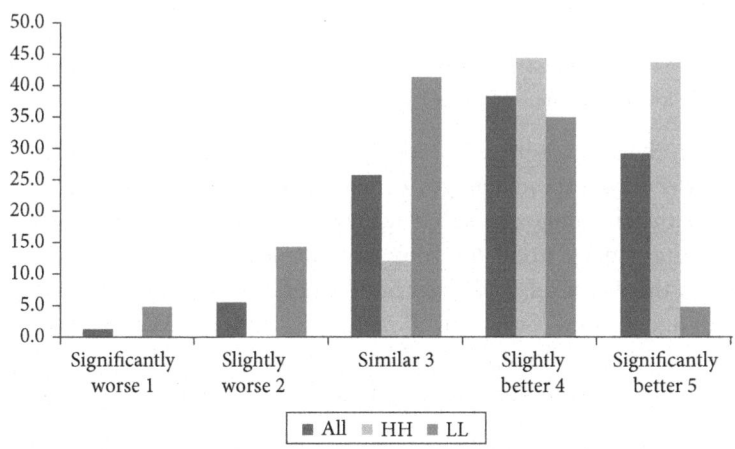

FIGURE 6.3 *Perceptions of market share changes*

companies to address what appear to be contradictions. Specifically, in the EY Report, it calls for: (1) balancing the extremes of the short term versus the long term; (2) local needs versus global capabilities; (3) entrepreneurial versus control; (4) risk versus scale; (5) affordable versus premium products; and (6) adaptability versus efficiency.[4]

One reason is the emergence of "dual-speed" markets, which are accentuated by granular growth. Paul Janelle, president director of Sampoerna, states: "You have to think locally. In Indonesia, the islands of the Archipelago are different economically and culturally. We look at our brand portfolio and we look at the economy of one city or one area, compared to another city, and taste preferences of adult smokers, and then we target our execution to meet consumer demand."

Disparity in expected economic development leads to variations in the timing of revenues and growth, creating some form of dilemma. Firms have to expect long-term profit and short-term growth, without compromising a profit focus. They have to balance the requirements of seeking growth in the short term and securing profits in the long term. Yves Pellegrino, corporate finance director at Danone, opines:[5]

> In the early stages, you need to invest more than you can extract margins from these markets. But, our view is that we need to move fairly quickly to what we call a "pay-as-you-go" system.
>
> Once you have reached that stage, then you can reinvest at the speed with which you generate margin—that is the most sustainable way. If you grow just for the sake of growing, then you will quickly find yourself in big trouble because you cannot replicate that everywhere on Earth. Your resources are always going to be limited, and you have to allocate them carefully. The pay-as-you-go system means that you give markets the ammunition and fuel for the business to grow by itself.

Another challenge is meeting local consumer needs in a way that does not undermine the advantages of leveraging global capabilities. This is likewise the challenge posed by localization. On the one hand, firms need to nurture a deep understanding of what local consumers want, often down to the city level, and must build their offering around those needs. But a singular focus on localization can risk much lower returns because the company cannot reap the full benefits of scale and scope economies. Paul Janelle, president director of Sampoerna, asserts:

> You have to think locally. In Indonesia, the islands of the Archipelago are different economically and culturally. We look at our brand portfolio, and

we look at the economy of one city or one area, compared to another city and taste preferences, and then we target our execution to meet consumer demand... they must be entrepreneurial and operate within a global corporate culture. Emerging Asia is a dynamic, fast-moving market that rewards an entrepreneurial approach to risk taking and decision making. Multinationals need to figure out how to empower this entrepreneurial mindset, while at the same time embedding it within a global corporate culture and set of values.

David Steer, managing director, East.West.SBS, and former president of Kraft Foods Russia, likewise adds: "With the stagnation in mature markets, emerging markets are under pressure to drive growth and make up for the shortfalls of Europe. Having good compliance is important, but the bureaucracy around it should not be unnecessarily burdensome."[6]

For as long as emerging markets grow and develop, contradictions as described will present dilemmas for firms as much as core strategies will be tested along their boundaries. It is essential, therefore, for firms to be aware of these contradictions and to prepare contingencies and resources for various scenarios. Such will be the difference in distinguishing higher and lower performance. Awareness will depend on reliable information and adequate resources, a topic discussed in the next section.

Secure data analytics and financial sources for investment

To keep track of a fast-changing environment, both data analytics and financial capital are critical. Without reliable analysis, environmental events can be misconstrued, leading to erroneous decisions. Without financial capital, or access to it, it will prove daunting if not impossible to lubricate a firm's activities. Thus, both constitute an important positioning decision.

Consider the activities of a Japanese multinational the EY team interviewed that has successfully penetrated emerging markets. According to the overseas general manager, the company prepares for any market entry with a comprehensive survey and selects their products based on "what will beat the competition." When market data prove intractable, they use its local employees to visit homes and conduct consumer surveys. This contrasts with the industry practice of employing outside market research companies. In Indonesia, the company employs its overseas Chinese-affiliated representative offices. Personalized interaction is perceived as critical for fine-tuning the requirements of any of the company's local products.

The CFO for China of a global food company suggests:

> Data are very important. But, I think an even more important challenge is how we can consolidate or convert raw data into information that is understandable to all key managers across all functions. If the data are too raw, they are useless because nobody can understand them. So, how do we do it? First, by consolidating all the different systems or legacy platforms into one using SAP, as well as selected KPIs… Second, we are able to gather our sales database through our own sales information systems… we also manage the data using an external service provider, specifically AC Neilson, that basically provides information on market share and category growth, helping us to quantify and be able to do our forecast in a much more accurate manner using a more scientific approach.

The diversity of consumers in developing countries accentuates the need for in-depth analysis. As noted by the CEO of an Indonesian consumer business unit,

> One of the things you need regarding putting in investments, because what you asked about was investments, the first thing you have to do is to invest in data. You have to have the data to understand, in the geographies, what social and economic standards people hold. You have to understand adjacent businesses. For instance, if mining is investing, when mining invests, a lot of people move in to the area. Those people that move can come from Java, they come with a certain preference in what they like to consume, so you have to have that information. So, you have to invest in data. It's about understanding the geographies, what's happening, what's the purchasing power of people according to area. You have to understand that in terms of data.

In our interviews, respondents reaffirmed that investments are essential for successfully sustaining their strategies. Investments, particularly by headquarters, also signal the level of commitment to local operations in emerging markets. On the contrary, if local operations are profitable, then investments from headquarters might not be as forthcoming. Hence, by way of positioning, these respondents also indicated that investments should not be viewed in global terms, but in terms of specific allocation to the local (emerging) market. As such, how did firms with varying performance differ?

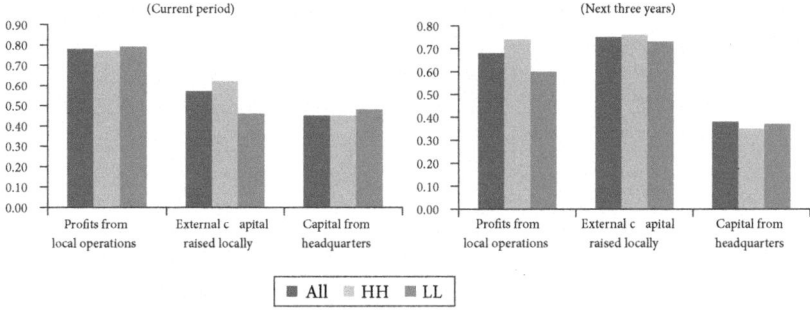

FIGURE 6.4 *Sources of financial resources (current vs. in three years)*

Higher performing firms are more likely to anticipate funding from *local operations* and *external capital*. This finding applies to both current and future (projected three years) operations. This finding suggests that higher performers have sufficient confidence in their local operations so that they see themselves as less dependent on headquarters for funding operations. Presumably because of this success, higher performers also see external capital as a source for local operations. In contrast, lower performing firms are less confident in securing local and external funds, and are consequently more reliant on headquarters. This raises the issue of how firms approach and prioritize emerging markets in terms of their total portfolio (Figure 6.4).

Attach high priority to emerging markets

As indicated in Chapter 1, the focus of this study is multinational firms, both from developed countries and from other countries in Asia, operating in emerging markets. It is not surprising that emerging markets are one of the important outlets for investment. As such, the next question aims to ascertain the importance of emerging markets relative to a firm's overall investment portfolio. How do firms with varying levels of performance perceive this importance?

In our survey, in contrast to lower performing firms, higher performing firms see emerging markets as more important and central to their planning and operations. Specifically, as analyzed and reported in an advance copy of the EY Report, "By 2017, emerging Asia will account for

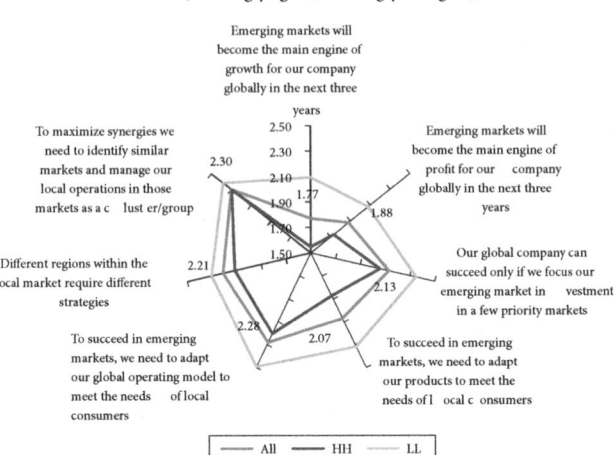

FIGURE 6.5   *Perceptions of the significance of emerging markets*

one-quarter of the global consumer products market and generate 38% of total consumer products growth."[7]

By this account, higher performing firms see emerging markets, taken as a whole, as an important profit sanctuary and an engine of growth and prosperity. Even so, the obverse does not apply for lower performing firms. Lower performers do not see emerging markets as less important. In fact, lower performers exhibit even more confidence in the potential of emerging markets across the spectrum, perhaps anticipating higher growth than the higher performers. Beyond perceptions of importance, strategic decisions need to be made on how to grow and expand these sectors (Figure 6.5).

Systematically pursue modes of expansion

An important element of strategic positioning is a firm's expansion mode. In our survey, we probed various paths to expansion, from local sales force to franchising to mergers and acquisitions. Our findings indicate that both higher and lower performing firms view mergers and acquisitions (with majority control) as the principal path to expansion in local operations. However, higher performing firms are more likely to invest in local operations, while lower performing firms prefer partnerships and alliances (Figure 6.6).

Kraft Malaysia Sdn. Bhd. is exemplary in terms of its systemic expansion strategy. A subsidiary of Mondolez International, Kraft Malaysia meticulously built its operations in Malaysia through mergers and acquisitions. Currently, Kraft Malaysia is the acknowledged market leader in Oreo Cookies, Maxwell House Coffee, among other products, in Malaysia. The company strategy honed through the years has been the acquisition of local companies, mirroring the success of its parent company (Mondolez) in the acquisition of Cadbury.[8]

Another company, JT International Berhad (JTI Malaysia), is equally renowned for its successful merger and acquisition track. A division of Japan Tobacco International, JT International Berhad expanded with the timely acquisition of Renault-Malaysia in 1999, and currently boasts eight Global Flagship Brands—Winston, Camel, Mild Seven, Benson & Hedges, Silk Cut, Sobranie, Glamour, and LD.[9]

Relatedly, higher performing firms operate in a wide range of retail formats (traditional, modern trade, ownership in exclusive retail outlets,

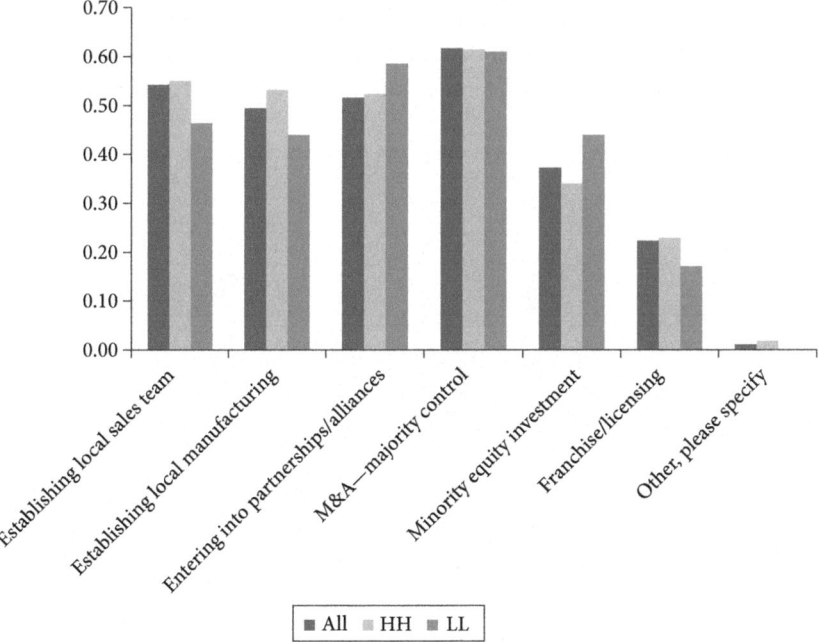

FIGURE 6.6 *Expansion modes in emerging markets*

and direct channels). Lower performing firms also operate in these formats, although not as extensively. Both sets of firms consider mergers and acquisitions as their primary expansion mode, although higher performing firms are more likely to build on local sales and manufacturing and their own distribution channels. These preferences for investing in local infrastructure, as opposed to widespread distribution outlets, underscore differences between higher and lower performing firms.

Another strategy to achieve profitable growth is the use of diverse distribution outlets. When Kelti China, a manufacturer of beauty and health products from Taiwan, embarked on the mainland, they were unsure of what might work with consumers.[10] Hence, the company adopted a multi-pronged approach, combining direct selling, the use of beauty salons as sales outlets, and even the judicious use of digital network channels. In doing so, the company was able to solicit key information from its targeted consumers and, in the process, calibrate its strategy to fit changing circumstances (Figure 6.7).

Among the notable accomplishments in distribution outlets is Cadbury India Ltd.[11] While supermarkets and hypermarkets now pervade India's consumer sectors, close to 98% of food is still purchased in 12 million neighborhood mom-and-pop outfits (*kirana*). Two challenges in this regard include having to distribute chocolate directly, which raises transit costs, and keep the chocolate at a cool temperature, otherwise it becomes perishable

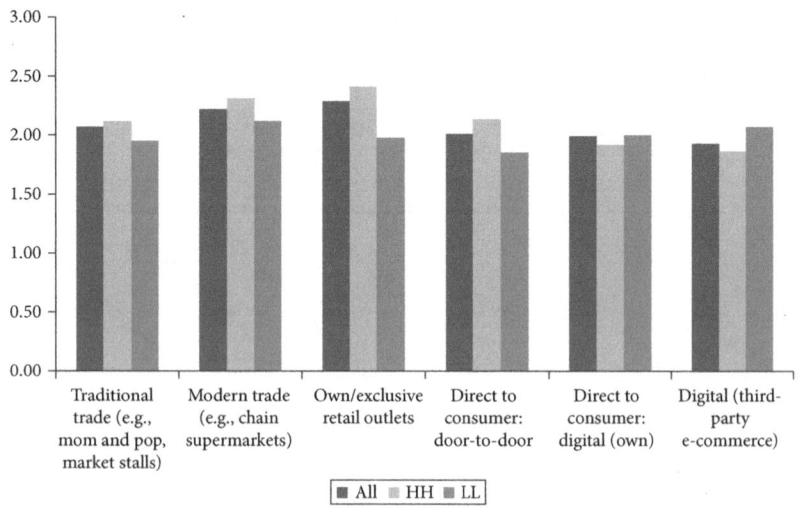

FIGURE 6.7   *Types of sales channels in emerging markets*

during the hot season. Cadbury circumvented these challenges by creating two central distribution channels to reduce costs, and an ingenious way of developing a cold chain system, inclusive of visi-coolers and chocolate dispensers, to maintain the proper temperature for the products.[12]

Summing up—appraising differences in strategic positioning

Table 6.1 summarizes our findings relating to strategic positioning. All in all, higher and lower performing firms exhibit marked differences in their basic approaches to growth. Consistent with the interviews, higher performing firms emphasize growth in revenue and operating profits, while lower performing firms focus on market share. Higher performing firms are also more likely to view their external environments as having more impact on operations than are lower performing firms. All firms, higher and lower performing ones, perceive greater importance and centrality of emerging markets in their operations. Differences in the views of uncertainty and volatility are important in that they are consequential. In the academic literature, differences in perceptions can lead not only to strategic choices, but also to decisions about implementation, such as the type of organizational structure and processes. Positioning choices are inextricably linked to what firms consider to be the principal drivers of a differentiation strategy—the topic of the next chapter.

TABLE 6.1 *Differentiating higher and lower performing firms in positioning*

Survey item	Higher performer (HH)	Lower performer (LL)
KPI (Current year)	Focus on revenue growth	Focus on market share
KPI (Next three years)	Focus on revenue growth and operating profits	Focus on market share and revenue growth
Perceptions of external environment	High environmental uncertainty and volatility	Low environmental uncertainty and volatility
Sources of finance	Profits from local operations and other external sources	Capital from HQ
Importance of emerging markets	Increased impact in the future	Decreased impact in the future
Expansion mode	M & A; establishing local sales and manufacturing	M & A; entering partnerships and alliances
Distribution channels	Own retail channels; trade; and direct channels	Direct sales; digital channels

Notes

1. Michael E. Porter, *Competitive Strategy* (New York: Free Press, 1980).
2. Al Ries and Jack Trout, *Positioning: A Battle for Your Mind* (New York: McGraw Hill, 2001), p. 5.
3. EY. Profit-or-lose. Balancing the growth-profit paradox for global consumer products companies and retailers in Asia's emerging markets. 2013. http://emergingmarkets.ey.com/profit-or-lose-2/.
4. The idea behind inconsistencies and dilemmas in emerging markets arising from transition is attributable to Andrew Cosgrove. This section largely adopts this perspective that is a part of a report, "Profit-or-lose: Balancing the growth-profit paradox for global consumer products companies and retailers in Asia's emerging markets," EYG no. EN0519; CSG/GSC2013/1164313; ED 1015 (2013):12–15.
5. EY. Profit-or-lose.
6. Ibid.
7. Ibid.
8. http://www.bloomberg.com/research/stocks/private/snapshot.asp?privcapId=33876198.
9. http://en.wikipedia.org/wiki/JTI_Macdonald#History.
10. http://www.kelti.com.cn. http://www.hll9.com/news/336.html; http://www.corpasia.net/hongkong/00157/financial/19/EN/ew00157_JDjmAcI264mH.pdf; http://www.nblife.com; and http://wenku.baidu.com/view/b157a6c75fbfc77da269b1bf.html
11. Adopted and synthesized from company documents including: http://www.ukessays.com/essays/marketing/marketing-report-on-cadbury-india-ltd-marketing-essay.php and http://en.wikipedia.org/wiki/cadbury.
12. http://www.confectionerynews.com/Processing-Packaging/Cadbury-develops-temperature-tolerant-chocolate.

7
Defining the Drivers of Profitable Growth

Abstract: *In this chapter, we discuss various drivers based on survey results and field interviews focusing on the differences between higher and lower performing firms. Our objective was to define fine-grained, micro-level decisions, using the following drivers of performance in the survey: (1) channels of competitive advantage; (2) strategies for future revenue growth; and (3) strategies for cost reduction. Although most, if not all, firms indicated that they pursued a differentiation strategy, there are various ways of reaching this objective and excelling in the process. Some differing characteristics among the firms include the following: (1) exploring all sources of competitive advantage; (2) assessing localization through affordable innovation; (3) exploiting sources of synergies; (4) scaling product categories, not products; and (5) exploring strategies for cost reduction.*

Park, Seung Ho, Gerardo R. Ungson, and Andrew Cosgrove. *Scaling the Tail: Managing Profitable Growth in Emerging Markets.* New York: Palgrave Macmillan, 2015. DOI: 10.1057/9781137538598.0016.

In the strategy literature, strategic positioning is strongly tied to drivers of performance. While positioning depicts a firm's planned alignment with the external environment in ways that bestow competitive advantage, the drivers specifically delineate operational and tactical decisions that support or enhance a given strategy.

In the strategy literature, the distinction between competitive strategy and competitive advantage is well delineated. Harvard guru Michael Porter emphasizes that strategic choices likewise relate to positioning decisions that firms might choose not to employ.[1] Strategy involves the primary placement of a firm relative to competitors and its environment. In contrast, gaining competitive advantage typically entails operational activities that support and sustain a primary strategy. In Porter's formulation, advantage is identified through a firm's value chain that depicts a firm's activities from its input of resources, its throughput function, and to its output and after-sales activities.[2]

Consistent with Porter's view and our objective of defining fine-grained, micro-level decisions, we operationalized the following drivers of performance in the survey: (1) channels of competitive advantage; (2) strategies for future revenue growth; and (3) strategies for cost reduction. Our findings and conclusions comprise the rest of this chapter.

Explore different sources of competitive advantage

Although most, if not all, firms indicated that they pursued a differentiation strategy, there are various ways of reaching this objective and excelling in the process. To sustain profitable growth over time, firms have to be vigilant about exploring *all* sources of competitive advantage. In view of the fast-changing competitive landscape of emerging economies, this can no longer be a discretionary activity, but a purposeful and meticulous exercise (Figure 7.1).

There are notable differences between higher and lower performing firms in this regard. Higher performing firms identify themselves as differentiators with the three top-ranked sources being *price point, product quality*, and *product innovation*. As described in the previous chapter, Cadbury India created visi-coolers to maintain the proper temperature for chocolate during the hot and humid seasons of India. The company also invented a form of chocolate that could circumvent the effects of hot climates for which it has filed a patent. Accordingly, Cadbury has held

Defining the Drivers of Profitable Growth 69

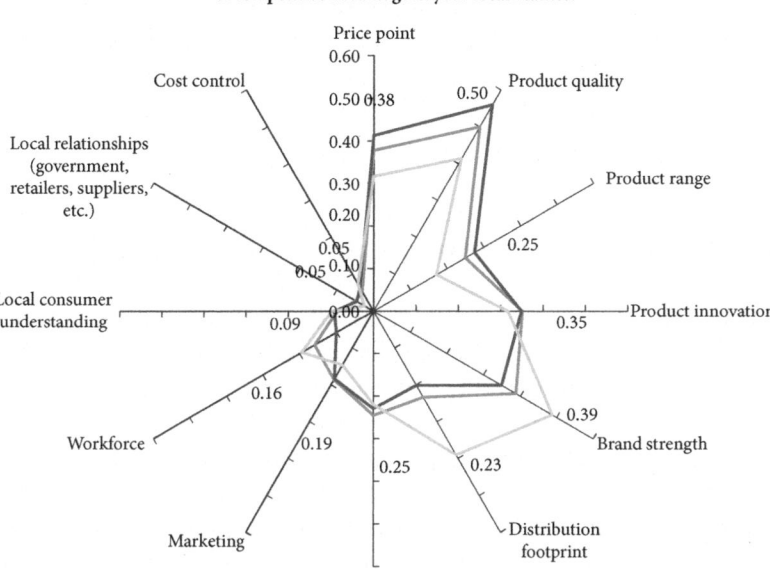

FIGURE 7.1 *Sources of competitive advantage in emerging markets*

onto its premium chocolate segment, despite intense competition from international and local firms.[3]

Similarly, Colgate Palmolive India, Ltd. has excelled in product innovation with its sensitivity toothpaste, mouthwash, and flavored products.[4] This accomplishment was initiated with a royalty-based agreement with Colgate Palmolive USA in 2002 that involved the development and exchange of technical know-how. Colgate Palmolive India now boasts product innovations, such as the first electric toothbrush in India, the Sensitive Pro-Relief Toothpaste that provides instant sensitivity relief, Colgate's 360 Sensitive Pro-Relief or its premium product, and Colgate Plax Complete Care Mouthwash.[5]

Interestingly, lower performing firms view *brand strength* and *distribution* as their relative competitive advantages, but score lower on product quality and product range. There are no significant differences between the groups in terms of local relationships and understanding, workforce, marketing, and sales service. Lower performing firms are pursuing a similar differentiation strategy, but do not rank these as strengths relative to higher performing firms (or relative to the total sample). Differentiation advantages are enhanced to the extent that firms can successfully address the requirements of the local markets that were previously nascent and simply flooded by trimmed-down features of a firm's standard product.

Assess localization through affordable innovation

The question that was posed throughout the field interviews and a theme that resonates throughout this book is: Given the emerging needs of local markets, how do firms balance global levering with local accommodation? In the past, the answer was a simple and successful one: examine the features of a differentiated product that match the needs of the local market, trim down whatever is necessary, and offer a lower and affordable price. Unfortunately, this formula can no longer work as well as expected. Local consumers have increased in terms of their expectations and sophistication, leading to much higher localization costs (and lower returns). The issue is compounded in that localization now extends beyond product offerings and covers expectations relating to the hiring of local talent.

Hence, can a firm meet the new requirements of localization, while also benefiting from scale and scope economies? The answer provided by high performance firms was yes, and the strategy used is what they termed "affordable innovation." To understand what the term entails, it is instructive to review the imperatives leading to its formulation.

The rationale behind affordable innovation is an incremental approach to studying the emerging needs of local markets while investing only in selected features, which include both the product and the local community, that comprise a defensible cost structure and an affordable price. One EY interviewee states:

> There are two dynamics behind affordable innovation. One is the consumer. The lower middle class/aspiring working classes are rising up and you want to capture them. And secondly, it is the competition—the Chinese, the Asians, the Middle Eastern companies—coming in with a good enough quality product at a cheap price.
>
> The Chinese like a lot of brands, but they are not yet brand loyal. With affordable innovation, however, you address the needs of 200 million people

on less than $2 per day in China, craft a profit objective, and then develop a firm portfolio... But with Asia, there is so much local affordable innovation, and to do that there is a cost. My gut tells me that in order to do things correctly, you really have to plunge into the local element and compete on the local side.

If you cede the market to locals, they will absorb it, and this only makes them bigger and perhaps global players in the future.

Another interviewee underscores the growing competitiveness of local firms as the rationale underlying affordable innovation: "Local players are more and more international ... they are increasing and exporting more... becoming competitive... You have to adapt the products... you have to accept less margin... and it is a shopper's market now... (aggressive promotions)."

Collectively, affordable innovation is an incremental strategy to address granular growth, uneven economic development, and rising local competition. However, it is also a departure from traditional strategy that emphasizes the leveraging of a global product. It also abrogates traditional thinking that the effective way to address consumers who are not mainstream is by trimming down features of the global product to arrive at an affordable price. Because consumers in previously unexplored niches have become more affluent and desire differentiated features, a new approach based on a new mindset is needed to accommodate their needs. While respondents expressed the need for affordable innovation, the question remains regarding strategies to reach these new segments as future revenue growth—a topic discussed in the next section.

Exploit sources of synergies for future growth

In tandem with affordable innovation, firms have to continue to focus on sources of synergies arising from marketing or merchandising strategies that can lead to future revenue growth. Profits are attained from higher prices, assuming that consumers consider the benefits from differentiation and are willing to pay a premium price for them. Firms can also benefit from cost reduction for so long as it does not jeopardize the product brand and image. Finally, economies can arise from scale and scope.

In our study, higher performing firms are proficient in employing these strategies in local markets: *raising prices, lowering costs,* and *utilizing new distribution channels.* Synergies from these strategies can continue to build on further competitive advantages. Lower performing firms emphasize expanding distribution, innovating existing products, and launching new services in current markets. The latter cannot or do not typically engage in premium pricing.

Prior to its ascendancy as the top producer in China's beverage industry, Kangshifu was considered inferior to its key competitor, Uni-President Enterprises.[6] However, following a temporary drop in supply for Uni-President products, Kangshifu seized the opportunity to flood the market with its products. Kangshifu's success partly derived from its broad distribution channels that extended through urban and rural areas. The company lived by its motto: "cultivate the channels and dominate the market." Because Uni-President opted not to compete by building distributorships, Kangshifu was able to reap scale economies and improve on its margins. In addition, brand awareness throughout China has been high and amplified further with Kangshifu's various diverse offerings.

BOX 7.1 *Building synergy through localization and distribution at Want Want China Holdings Limited*

> Think of rice crackers, chewing gum, pastries, nuts, and carbonated drinks in China and you will probably find its branded label as the Want Want China Holdings Limited. The company was incorporated in 1962 with its corporate headquarters located in George Town, Cayman Islands. Unassumingly, it is publicly listed on the Hong Kong Stock Exchange, but with a simple ticker symbol "00151." However, do not let its unpretentious public figure mislead you: it is one of the most successful companies in China.
>
> Its competitive strategies anchor two goals to build synergy: localization and distribution. All personnel are locally recruited, and this group includes several technical officers. The company then embarks on a systematic training program to ensure that local tastes are considered as a major input into strategic decisions. Raw materials are produced locally. Want Want sees localization as the key to cost reduction, as well as a way to reach the local targeted population. Even with research and development in Taiwan, the company makes quite certain that local tastes are examined and tested in its various product offerings.
>
> In addition, the company touts the benefits of a strong distribution system. Discounts and incentives are given to the more successful

dealers. To maintain dealers' commitment, the company promises first delivery to excellent dealers who might not have had very good performance in earlier periods due to limited supply. Moreover, the company measures performance based on actual sales, not overstock. In all of these activities, the company encourages dealers to sell in rural areas that might not be targeted by competitors.

Source: Company documents including: http://www.jxfqs.com/Item/Show.asp?m=112&d=50; http://www.jxcn.cn/34/2005-9-8/30005 51@178747.htm; http://en.wikipedia.org/wiki/Want_Want_China; http://www.bloomberg.com/research/stocks/snapshot/snapshot.asp?capId=882034.

The pattern reflects efficiency in channel management. Higher performing firms utilize premium pricing and capitalize on new distribution channels, while also reducing costs. In contrast, lower performing firms expand their existing distribution channels, instead of building new ones. Innovating new products and refining current offerings reflect strategies to enhance the differentiated features of their products, although limited in terms of commanding premium prices.

In all, higher performing firms are able to grow more aggressively with profit pools from well-differentiated product offerings. Procter & Gamble Hygiene and Health Care, a manufacturer of health care and feminine hygiene products in India, fared well against a major competitor, Johnson & Johnson (J & J), with its introduction of a high-quality "dry feel" benefit called Whisper that J & J could not match, despite the fact that the latter was the first entrant in this area in India (J & J ultimately reduced its price for its Stayfree product to defend its market position). Among lower performing firms, differentiation to the point of defensible price premiums remains a goal, but is not yet a reality (Figure 7.2).[7]

These findings confirm patterns that are foreshadowed in the preceding section. Higher performing firms consider raising prices, reducing costs, and utilizing new distribution channels as engines of future growth. In contrast, lower performing firms view the expansion of current distribution channels, innovating existing products, and realigning marketing spending as the key drivers. Findings also confirm that lower performing firms are not able, as yet, to raise prices or expand into new distribution channels. Collectively, these differences can be attributed to basic capabilities: while the pursuit of differentiation applies to both

Scaling the Tail

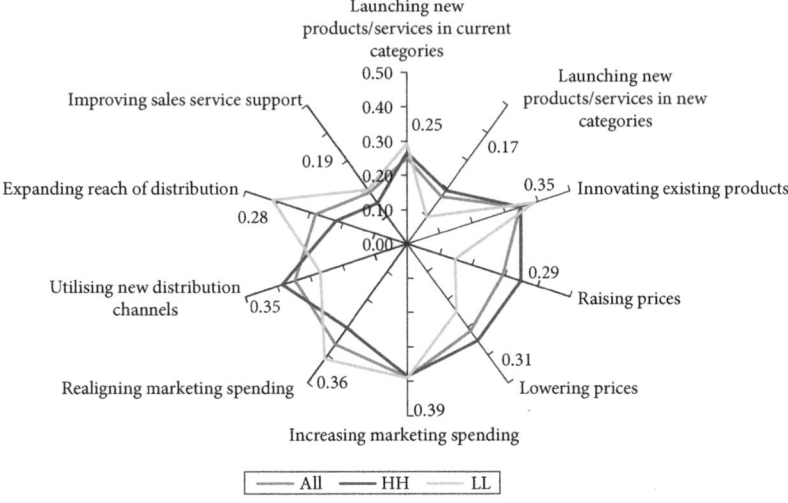

FIGURE 7.2 *Drivers of revenue growth in emerging markets*

types of firms, higher performing firms, by virtue of reputation and experience, are able to command premium pricing and growth strategies relative to their lower performing counterparts.

Scale up product categories, not products

In Michael Porter's *Competitive Strategy*, the selection of a firm's scope of operation comprises a fundamental part of strategic positioning. In our survey, we probed the following dimensions of scope: (1) few or multiple product categories; (2) low versus premium pricing; (3) local versus global brand propositions; (4) the use of R&D as local leverage; (5) internal manufacturing versus importing; and (6) local versus national priorities.

Compared to other firms, higher performing firms (68% vs. 49% for lower performing firms) tend to (1) participate in multiple product categories; (2) create new product categories; (3) offer premium-priced products; (4) sell these products on a global scale; (5) use global value propositions consistently; and (6) capitalize on local product platforms. This pattern accentuates the differences in varying performance, that is, lower performing firms tend to focus more on 1–2 product categories (41% vs. 32% for higher performing firms). Moreover, higher performing firms are more apt to create new product categories than lower performing firms (53% vs. 44%). These findings corroborate those obtained from our field interviews. As indicated, the employment of multi-brands was, in part, a central strategic arsenal to accommodate the multi-faceted preferences of an emergent affluent middle-class sector (Figures 7.3–7.5).

Consider the case of Hindustan Unilever India, whose detergent business spans multiple segments in response to previous nascent sectors, including premium (Surf-HUL, Ariel-P&G), mid-price (Rin-HUL, Henko, Tide-P&G), and popular segments (Ghari, Wheel-HUL, Nirma, Mr. White). What is particularly impressive is that these brands account for 15%, 40%, and 45% of the market share, respectively, or 60% of the total market. The remaining 40% is occupied by regional and small unorganized players.[8]

This use of multi-brands is noted by the China CFO of a global snacks company:

> I think our focus would remain on our power brands. If you look back to the business four years ago, we had more than 30 brands in our portfolio and some of the brands were very, very small in volume. Some of the brands were basically bleeding, which means incurring losses, and some of the brands had very low margins. We started a portfolio review four years ago and came to a decision to focus on our strategy to invest in nine power brands. That focus on a big, big drive had a very, very significant result in the turnaround.

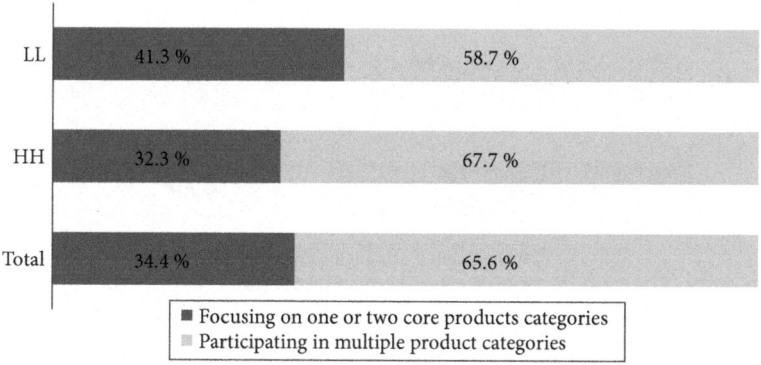

FIGURE 7.3 *Strategic focus on product categories*

Yet, in our view, the extreme forms of both approaches are not appropriate in emerging markets, and should be avoided. Uncritical globalization leaves open the possibility that a product will not be suited to the local market, and overlocalization can also lead to significantly high transferability costs. The need to balance both approaches resonated in our interviews. The Indonesia business unit CEO stated:

> We're a bit of an anomaly. We acquired some fantastic local brands, which have solid, solid brand foundations. So, what we have here in our brand portfolio is the best that exists in Indonesia. And what we've managed to do is we brought in international expertise in marketing, sales, systems, and information systems, and have been able to take an excellent brand foundation and bring it to the next level.

Consider the multi-branding strategy of Cadbury India: its relative competitiveness against Nestle is the result of a solid and reputable brand image that was nurtured for over six decades. It ranks among the best known chocolate brands; in fact, Cadbury in India is so well known that it is synonymous with chocolate, much in a similar way that xeroxing is associated with the Xerox Corporation. Cadbury's brands comprise a comprehensive portfolio: Dairy Milk (flagship), Dairy Milk & Fruit and Nuts, Dairy Milk Roasted Almonds, Dairy Milk Crackles, 5-Star, 5-Star Crunchy, Perk, Gems, Shots, Eclairs, Bournville, and Dairy Milk Silk.[9]

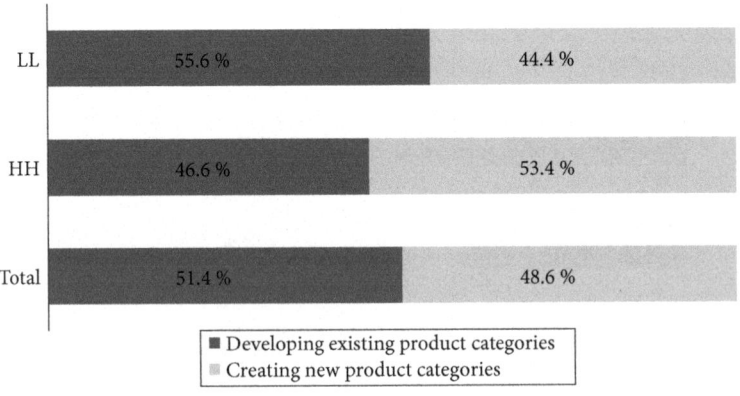

FIGURE 7.4 *Strategies for product category development*

BOX 7.2 *Nestle's approach to multi-tiered branding*

Among the stalwarts of foreign multinationals operating in emerging markets is Nestle. Founded in 1866, the company is headquartered in Switzerland and ranks among the top-tiered global leaders in nutrition. Its motto, "Good Food, Good Life," is "to provide consumers with the best tasting, most nutritious choices in a wide range of food and beverage categories, and eating occasions, from morning to night."

Nestle's strategy in emerging markets is no less ambitious: it seeks to be the leader in nutritional snacks unsurpassed in quality and reputation. In China and India, in particular, the company has already achieved major performance milestones. Its brand strategy is a multi-tiered platform that targets every market segment, from the poor to the affluent. Its approach to the growing middle class is noteworthy by way of numerous brands. The emphasis on building on product categories is consistent with scaling up in order to flank particular segments.

Multi-tiered brand portfolio in India:

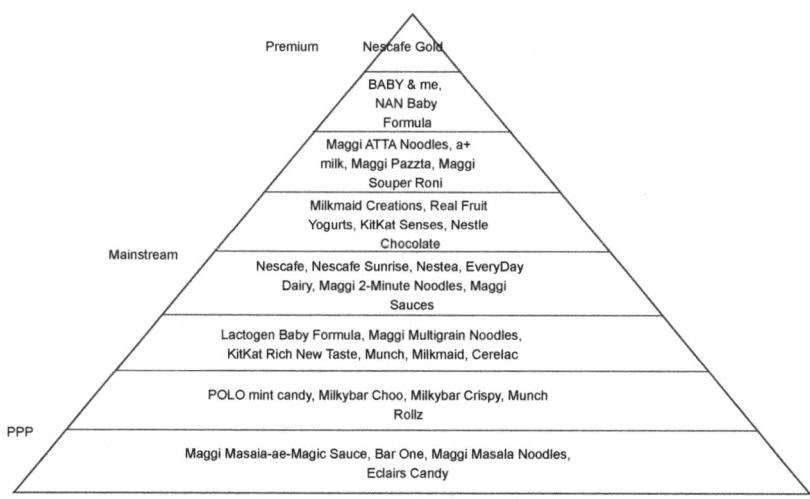

Multi-tiered brand portfolio in China:

Chinese urban household annual income ('000 RMB)	Dairy & Nutrition	Coffee	Beverage	Culinary	Confection	Ice cream	Hsu Fu Chi	Yinlu	Waters	Cereals	Pet food
Global Affluent >250 (6% of pop.)	NAN H.A. Formula NAN Formula	Nespresso Dolce Gusto		Taitaile Condensed Soup Taitaile Sesame Oil Maggi Seasoning	Aero Chocolate	Mövenpick			S. Pellegrino Perrier	Fitness	Purina Pro Plan
Mass Affluent 125–250 (12% of pop.)	Elder Milk Flavored Condensed Milk Lactogen Formula	Flavored Bottled Coffee Nescafe Gold Nescafe Flavored Canned Coffee	Milo	Taitaile Chicken Juice Seasoning Maggi Chicken Essence	KitKat (Bowl Pack) Fruit Candy (Large Pack) KitKat (Single Pack)	Dreyer's Mega			Acqua Panna Deep Spring Bottled Water	Cheerios	Purina Cat Chow Purina Hi Pro
Upper Middle Class 50–125 (39% of pop.)	Canned Condensed Milk Full-Fat Milk Powder	Nescafe 1+2 (Large Box) Nescafe (Glass Bottle) Nescafe Coffe-Mate (Glass Bottle)	Nestea Fruit Flavored Vitamin C Drinks (Large Pack)	Haoji Chicken Essence (Small Pack) Taitaile Chicken Essence (Small Pack)	Chocolate Wafer (Large Pack)	Nestle Drumstick Nestle Cube Nestle Home	Muffin Soft Nougat Peanut Nougat	Canned Flavored Congee	Yunnan Mountain Bottle Water Waterman Bottled Water	Nesvita (Large Pack)	Purina Friskies Purina Dog Chow
Lower Middle Class 30–50 (22% of pop.)	Child Milk Powder Sweetened Milk Powder Carnation Milk Alternative	Nescafe 1+2 (Small Box)	Fruit Flavored Vitamin C Drinks (Small Pack)	Taitaile Veg Essence Taitaile Soy Sauce	Chocolate Wafer (Single Pack)	Nestle Chocolate Stick Nestle Milk Stick	Roll Cookie Crisp Candy	Canned Mixed Congee Bottle Peanut Milk	Pure Life Bottled Water Pure Life Barreled Water	Nesvita (Small Pack)	
Poor <30 (21% of pop.)				Taitaile Food Essense	Fruit Candy (Small Pack)	Nestle Rice Cake Ice Cream	Caramel Treats				

Source: A modified narrative and the two figures on brands are taken from two presentations: "Nestle in Greater China: Winning in the New Reality," by Roland Decorvet, Chairman and CEO of Nestle Greater China and "Nestle in India: Winning in the New Reality," by Helio Waszyk, Chairman and Managing Director of Nestle India, Nestle Investor Seminar, Shanghai, September 25, 2012.

Explore strategies for cost reduction

Pursuing brand differentiation is neither inconsistent nor mutually exclusive with cost reduction. On the one hand, cost reduction should not denigrate the differentiated features of a product that becomes unacceptable to consumers; however, differentiation cannot be so costly that it erodes profit margins. In the survey, higher performing firms employ the following two sources for cost reduction: savings from centralization of procurement and manufacturing efficiencies. Lower performing firms focus on outsourcing and lean manufacturing. Higher performing firms are more likely to rely on internal factors and sources for developing competency whereas lower performing firms favor external or outsourcing venues. This reliance on internal versus external sources of cost reduction is what differentiates higher from lower performing firms. This might reflect the perceived amount of control exercised by these firms, in which higher performing firms perceive more control over their internal operations than lower performing firms.

When one examines the success of Lian Jiang Ching Luh Shoes, Ltd., in China, it is easy to forget the challenges that it faced in becoming a market leader.[10] Founded in September 2002, the company is a wholly owned subsidiary (Taiwan-based firm) and a subcompany of the Ching Luh Group. The latter is the traditional OEM provider in the footwear industry with a reputation for being a cost leader. Ching Luh initially capitalized on lower operating costs in Fujian, as well as incentives provided by the Chinese government for foreign investors. It also took advantage of cultural similarities between Taiwan and China, notably the language. Interestingly, the company was among many Taiwanese footwear firms that took advantage of South Korea's inability to keep up with attractive, but lower cost, shoes. Eventually, when labor costs in China started to rise, Ching Luh responded by moving some of its operations to Vietnam and Indonesia.

Differences between higher and lower performers are likewise evident in a firm's ability to defend premium pricing. Higher performing firms have relatively more power in establishing product differentiation than lower performing firms (51% vs. 46%). With respect to global versus local brand propositions, it is notable that lower performing firms rely more on global brands (51%) than do higher performing firms (37%). This suggests that higher performing firms might have already successfully introduced and modified their global brands, which then capitalize on local refinements to leverage their market position.

Procter and Gamble's marketing of its uber brand, Whisper, is a classic case of brand building and management. Advertisements featured mothers counseling their daughters on the proper use and benefits of sanitary napkins. Previously, such an area was not touched in India. A website was built for the brand. Even so, the success of P&G's campaign erased the stigma attached to sanitary napkins.[11]

As the chief customer officer of a global personal care company notes, "We focus on the top 30 markets in the world, which is about 85% of our business. We strive to understand where the best practices are in different markets, then turn those into repeatable models...our job is to understand each of these markets, and they are quite different, but then to apply our global expertise to find ways of determining how execution can be performed well." On the contrary, lower performing firms might rely more on a "push" strategy to secure market goals and objectives with respect to brand penetration.

In the case of Mondolez China, the company employs a combination of global and local approaches, depending on brand strength and potential coverage. According to Swee Leng Ng, CFO of Mondolez China (and former CFO of Kraft Foods China), the company leverages global brands with global innovations, which include improving the product's ingredients, fashioning a new marketing strategy, introducing the GBC concept, and refining the media concept. Nevertheless, the company has also modified the product to accommodate local tastes. Mr. Ng reports:

> We made it less sweet in China because the Chinese believe that sweetness is not good for your health and not good for children. When you see our products in China, you will notice that we have green tea and other fruit flavours, such as strawberry, pineapple... We have also introduced the snack pack, the bulk pack, the go packs, the gift packs, and even the tin packs. China has now become the second biggest market in the world after the United States.[12]

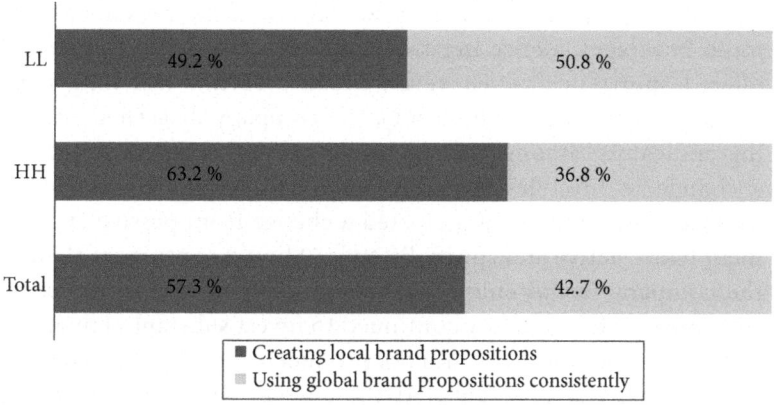

FIGURE 7.5 *Strategies for local brand positioning*

Herbalife might constitute one of the best examples combining shrewd skill with fortuitous circumstances.[13] Before finessing its direct-selling model, the company first sold its products in traditional retail stores in China. After being granted the first direct-selling license in China, Herbalife began to increase its national scope from initial forays in Suzhou and Nanjing in the Jiangsu province. Fortuitously, the concept of "herbal life" in China comports well with traditional Chinese medicine that is based on herbal drugs. This means "natural, healthy, and ecological." Not content at capitalizing on the direct association between its company name and China's traditional medicine, Herbalife enhanced its appeal with a television advertisement featuring a famous football star Messi who demonstrated skills in ping pong, a traditional Chinese sport. In this and other ways, Herbalife was especially adept at combining its standard product with an immersion in the Chinese culture.

The experience of Malaysia' beverage king, FNBM, is instructive in this regard (see Box 7.3).

BOX 7.3 *Learning in Malaysia's FNBM*

For more than a century, Malaysia's FNBM had taken deep pride in its knowledge of the local market. Its intimacy with local communities provided the company with a distinct advantage over foreign multinationals, despite the allure of foreign beverages for locals. When its iconic brand, 100Plus, was introduced, hardly anyone in the local community was aware of the benefits of isotonic beverages. Reflecting this condition, no other competitor offered sports drinks. However, because FNBM had long been engaged in the local community, the company discerned emerging indicators among its Malaysian consumers that suggested a change in lifestyles that resonated with trends in developed markets. The company anticipated a change from passive engagement to an "active and sporty lifestyle." Should consumers change, the company would enjoy first mover advantages. Convinced of such merits, the company continued to invest substantial financial and marketing resources into the product, even when the isotonic product was not profitable. At the current time, the company's belief in the product and its knowledge of local consumers' tastes has been validated. Its report states: "Today, 100Plus is the number one isotonic drink brand in Malaysia. An added bonus is that 100Plus is also Halal certified, ensuring the participation of its Malaysian Muslim consumers, who know that the drink is alcohol-free. It is also the only drink that is officially endorsed by the National Sports Council of Malaysia."

Source: Adapted from company documents including: http://fraserandneave.com/; quotes from "Coke Suffers Brand Backlash," *Asia's Media & Marketing Newspaper*, January 2009; "Soft Drinks in Malaysia," *Datamonitor*, April 2011, p. 14.

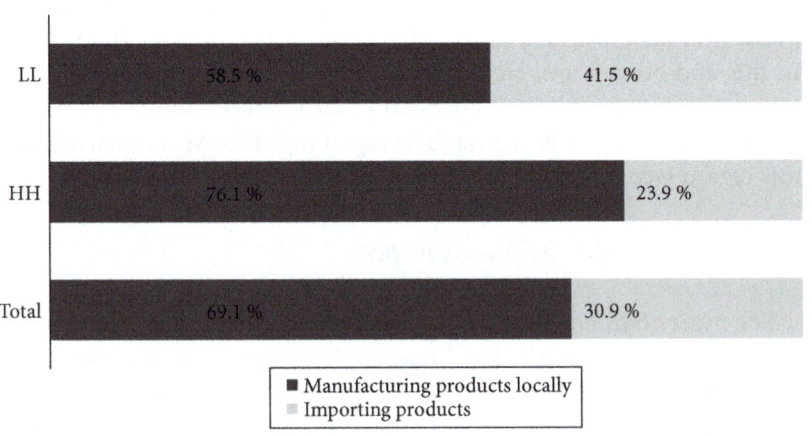

FIGURE 7.6   *Strategies for local product sourcing*

The decision to source local manufacturing or import products also reflects localization advantages. Specifically, higher performing firms manufacture products locally (76%) versus lower performing firms (59%). Partly as a consequence, lower performing firms (42%) import more products than higher performing firms (24%). Regarding the use of local research and development for product innovations or enhancement, there are no discernible differences between higher and lower performing firms (Figures 7.6 and 7.7).

For one consumer products interviewee, local investment is an imperative, not a discretionary decision: "One of the opportunities to compete with local players is very simple. Companies must either invest in China in terms of manufacturing or in Southeast Asia...when you invest in China, then you benefit from the ACTA Agreement between China and Southeast Asia. The second possibility is to invest in local manufacturing in Southeast Asia...the other way is to acquire local players with manufacturing sites and then benefit from their manufacturing costs and be able to propose cheaper products, but at reasonable gross market."[14] This imperative for localization is held in opposition to globalization, which is typically understood as the wholesale adoption of a generic business model to reduce the costs of transferability (see Box 7.4).

BOX 7.4 *Globalization and localization—when is too much or too little?*

Among marketers and strategists, there is the allure of global brands, as well as leveraging global presence by virtue of a firm's worldwide reputation. However, globalization has to be tempered by a sensitivity and accommodation of local needs and preferences. Given the changing competitive landscape, the key is to find an optimal balance between globalization and localization. If the scale tips excessively toward globalization, there is the risk that local consumers will reject the product because it is not compatible with their lifestyle patterns. There is the added risk that the product, while attractive, might be unaffordable. Too much localization or customization, on the contrary, reduces the benefits of economies derived from offering a "standard" product.

How can firms approach this problem such that some type of optimal balance is achieved? In this study, we found that current conditions, notably the preferences of Asia's surging middle class, have tilted the balance slightly in favor of localization. In fact, localization goes beyond product offerings; it permeates the selection of local managers, the design of management systems, the training of managers to ensure local adaptation, and the selective delegation of marketing plans and programs.

Even the entrenched belief that global strategies are best employed by strong and powerful firms with global reputations has become questioned. Consider the case of Google, a firm that is as global as any firm with a "standard" product. In China, the company faced difficulties with the government's censorship policies, privacy issues, and even unanticipated hacking incidents.[a]

Localization is the new imperative not only because of changing consumer preferences that are predicated on local culture, but also because of the rise of strong local companies. Google faces formidable competition from Baidu in China and from Yandex in Russia. McDonalds might be the world's most popular fast-food restaurant, but it did not fare well against competition from Philippines's Jollibee that had successfully crafted a local strategy based on taste, location, reputation, familial values, and local connections.

While traditional marketing tends to view market segments in terms of maps or markets, adapting a local perspective means viewing market segments in terms of the people who reside there.[b] It is not all surprising that John Quelch, a former Harvard professor and dean of CEIBS, and Katherine Jocz, a former Harvard researcher, propose an examination of local needs from a "psychological perspective." This approach relies heavily on psychographic and demographic methods of assessing the deep underlying preferences of local consumers that are rooted in the local culture. Taken altogether, this does not diminish the importance and strength of global brands, but emphasizes that attention to local needs has taken a central position in a firm's strategy, particularly when attending to the rising middle-class sectors in emerging markets.

Source: Examples (note a) are drawn from John Quelch and Katherine Jocz, *All Business Is Local: Why Place Matters More Than Ever in a Global, Virtual World* (New York: Portfolio/Penguin, 2012). The second note (b) is based on a personal conversation with Richard Steers, formerly with the University of Oregon.

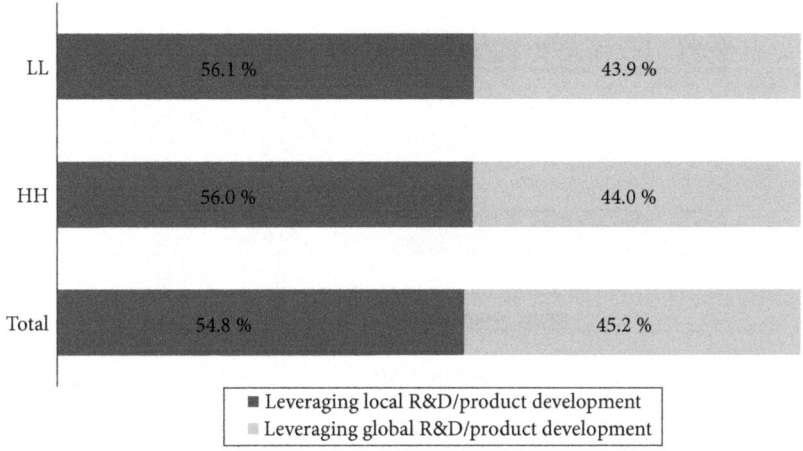

FIGURE 7.7   *Strategies for local product development*

Want Want China Holdings Limited established a research and development department in which extensive research and experimentation takes place. The company focuses on product innovation that combines nutritional studies of its numerous cracker products with close attention being paid to changes in China's food market. Currently, among its 130 products in the country, the company is distinguished for its snow cakes and Hot-Kid milk. While based in Taiwan, the company places high priority on its China market, as reflected in general terms in the next exhibit.[15]

Similarly, the international market leader of a Japanese food company states:

> Utilizing the technological prowess of the mother lab in Japan, we develop products that match local tastes, aligning brands with local tastes, as well. The company's most popular product is available in all countries. However, we also develop more high value-added products, such as flavor seasonings, complete menu seasoning mixes, instant noodles, etc., in each country or region. In this way, we differ from many global giants, which tend to offer only "global products" and "global brands."

To what extent are firms able to extend sales beyond their local market segments? In the survey, higher performing firms are able to sell more nationally (62%) relative to lower performing firms (48%). Perhaps at a point of transition, lower performing firms are still

86   Scaling the Tail

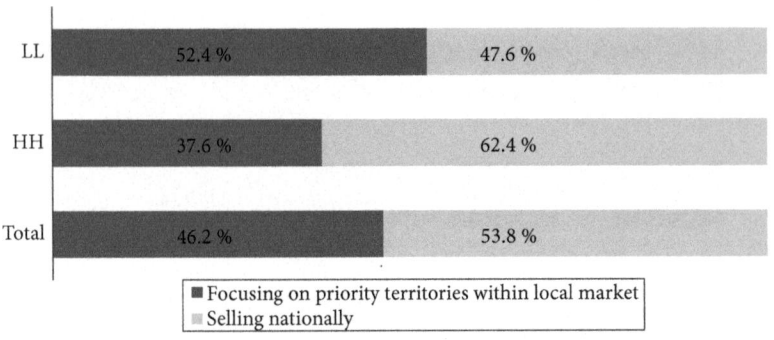

FIGURE 7.8   *Strategies for local product sales*

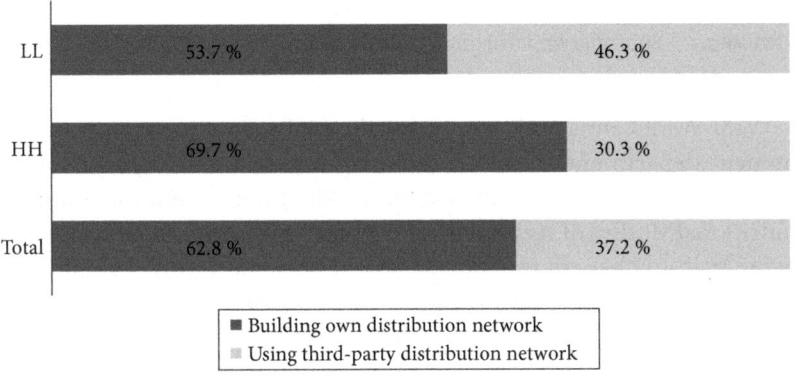

FIGURE 7.9   *Strategies for local product distribution*

confined to market niches whereas higher performing firms are able to leverage strengths arising from their local sales to national markets (Figure 7.8). PT Cahaya Kalbar TBK, a pioneer in Indonesia's vegetable and specialty oils for beverage and food confectionary industries, maintained its local market leadership with a focus on vegetable oils, local manufacturing, and an awareness of consumers' tastes and consumption patterns.[16]

Finally, higher performing firms are more capable of building their own (proprietary) distribution channels (70%) whereas lower performing firms rely more on third-party distribution networks (46%) (Figure 7.9). PT Multi Bintang Indonesia, a manufacturer of beer and nonalcholic beverages, focuses on building selective distributorships to

Which of the following cost reduction measures does your company consider the most important tools for improving margins?

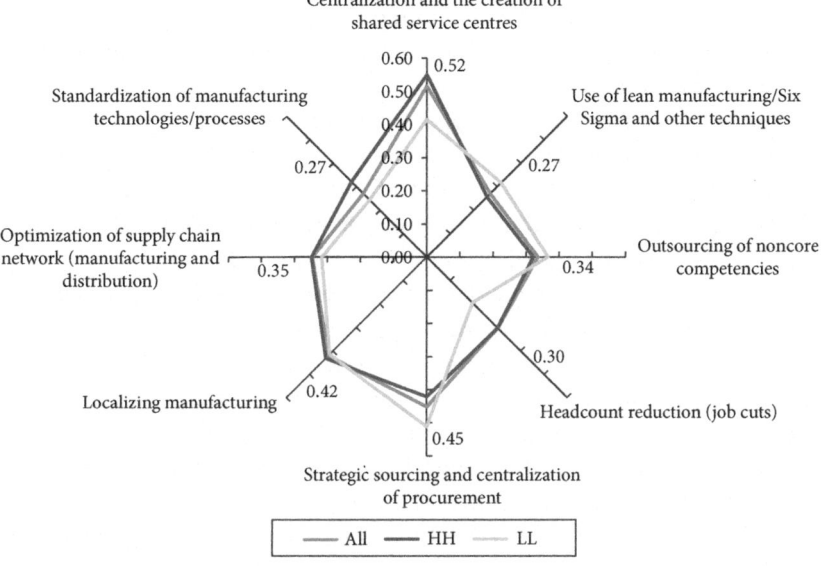

FIGURE 7.10   *Strategic drivers for cost reduction*

broaden its reach to older and younger consumers. Currently, the company operates on multiple channels and caters to first- and second-tier cities.[17] Our survey findings reflect the relative market power of higher performers and extends their scaling capabilities.

Summing up—defining the drivers of profitable growth

The second element of the P-E-C Framework is exploring drivers of competitive advantage. Firms have a myriad of choices for how to build advantages, with some more consequential than others. From the survey, higher and lower performing firms have clear and distinct differences in their fundamental tactics, even while pursuing a similar differentiation strategy. Consistent with interview findings, higher performing firms stake positions in multiple product categories or brand portfolios, command premium prices, employ a wider distribution footprint with new outlets, and are more likely to emphasize local manufacturing and research and development than lower performing firms. Higher performing firms offer stronger differentiation advantages, while lower performing firms perceive advantages as arising from more focused but lower-cost products (Figure 7.10).

Both sets of firms see advantages deriving from owning their distribution channels, although higher performing firms define their priority territories as national, as opposed to domestic/regional, which is the favored placement by lower performing firms (see Table 7.1).

Consistent with strategic positioning, higher and lower performing firms have adopted strategic drivers that reflect their desired advantages in differentiation and cost leadership. Higher performing firms employ price points and product quality to underscore their differentiation positions. In contrast, lower performing firms seek cost advantages in distribution, emphasizing the brands of current products, realigning marketing expenses, and outsourcing. In terms of localization, higher performing firms are more likely to focus on headcounts for cost reduction, but prefer decentralized activities for their local management, in contrast to more centralized locus of control by lower performing firms (Table 7.2). We defer a full discussion of localization to the next chapter.

TABLE 7.1 *Diferentiating higher and lower performing firms in positioning*

Survey item	Higher performer (HH)	Lower performer (LL)
Product focus	Multiple product categories	One or two core product categories
Future plans for new products	Create new product categories	Develop existing product categories
Differentiation/Cost	Emphasis on selling premium-priced products	Emphasis on selling low cost products
Geographical scope	Global	Domestic
Manufacturing focus	Local manufacturing	Local manufacturing plus imports
R & D organization	Local	Local
Priority territories	National	Regional
Distribution channels	Own distribution channels	Own distribution channels, but also alliances with third-party partners

TABLE 7.2 *Differentiating higher and lower performing firms in drivers*

Survey item	Higher performer (HH)	Lower performer (LL)
Sources of competitive advantage	Price points; product quality	Distribution; brand strength
Growth strategies	Raising prices for high-end products; utilizing new distribution channels	Expanding distribution channels; realigning marketing expenses
Cost reduction strategies	Centralized functions and activities; shared resources; headcount	Outsourcing; strategic sourcing
Localization focus	Headcount	Headcount; product range; supplier management
Locus of control	Decentralized	Centralized

Notes

1. Michael E. Porter, "What is strategy?" *Harvard Business Review,* November–December, 1996:1–20. http://weaddvalue2.web12.hubspot.com/Portals/188908/docs/hbr.what%20is%20strategy.pdf.
2. Michael E. Porter, *Competitive Advantage: Creating and Sustaining Superior Performance* (New York: Free Press, 1985).
3. http://www.confectionerynews.com/Processing-Packaging/Cadbury-develops-temperature-tolerant-chocolate.
4. http://www.funderuniverse.com/company-histories/colgate-palmolive-company-history/.
5. Ibid. See section "Basic toothpaste loses sparkle as buyers seek extra benefits."
6. See http://q.stock.sohu.com/hk/gg/n0028177o.shtml, http://www.irasia.com/listco/hk/tingyi/profile.htm, and http://www.cs.com.cn/gg/03/200811/t20081121_1661708.htm.
7. http://books.google.com.hk/books?id=auCt2-LPnLkC&pg=PA1975&lpg=PA1975&dq=P%26G+sanitary+napkin+innovation&source=bl&ots=niOFCqxIEW&sig=28A4LtdgojXR592f19PTITNQUP0&hl=zh-CN&sa=X&ei=A46bUbPUO8bliwLf3YDACA&ved=0CDUQ6AEwATge#v=onepage&q=P%26G%20sanitary%20napkin%20innovation&f=false.
8. See http://ankitmarketing.blogspot.com/2012/011/detergent-wars-nirma-wheel-and-ghari.html.
9. http://www.indiainfoline.com/markets/company/background/company-profile/mondelez-india-foods-ltd/244.
10. See http://www.104.com.tw/jb/104i/cust/view?c=383a4226445c3f6840583b1d1d1d1d5f24437323189j56 and http://www.chingluh.com.

11. http://books.google.com.hk/books?id=auCt2-LPnLkC&pg=PA1975&lpg=PA1975&dq=P%26G+sanitary+napkin+innovation&source=bl&ots=niOFCqxIEW&sig=28A4LtdgojXR592f19PTITNQUPo&hl=zh-CN&sa=X&ei=A46bUbPUO8bliwLf3YDACA&ved=0CDUQ6AEwATge#v=onepage&q=P%26G%20sanitary%20napkin%20innovation&f=false.
12. EY. "Profit-or-lose. Balancing the growth-profit paradox for global consumer products companies and retailers in Asia's emerging markets." 2013. http://emergingmarkets.ey.com/profit-or-lose-2/.
13. Information extracted and narrative adopted from the following sources: http://www.herbalife.cn; http://www.herbalife.com; http://www.herbalife.cn; http://www.chinadaily.com.cn/english/doc/2005-1/27/content_412659.htm; http://finance.qq.com/a/20070118/000485.htm; and http://www.fortunechina.com/management/c/2011-05/31/content_58181.htm.
14. The ACTA (Anti-Counterfeiting Trade Agreement) is a multinational treaty to establish international standards for intellectual property rights enforcement targeting counterfeit goods, generic medicines, and copyright infringement on the Internet. *Source*: Wikipedia (http://en.wikipedia.org/wiki/Anti-Counterfeiting_Trade_Agreement).
15. http://www.jxfqs.com/Item/Show.asp?m=112&d=50 and http://www.jxcn.cn/34/2005-9-8/30051@178747.htm.
16. http://www.cahayakalbar.com/.
17. http://www.euromonitor.com/beer-in-indonesia/report.

8
Co-aligning Strategies with Management Structures and Systems

Abstract: *There are key differences between higher and lower performing firms in regard to their approaches to execution: (1) what to centralize or decentralize; (2) recognizing external barriers to execution; (3) knowing the internal barriers to implementation; (4) investing in local human capital; and (5) creating a performance-based corporate culture. In all, higher performing firms are more likely to delegate authority to local management whom they regard as having good ability and competence. Lower performing firms do not consider their local management in the same regard. Higher performing firms see external barriers that limit both demand and supply. Lower performing firms see regulation and poor infrastructure in general as barriers. Finally, higher performing firms regard an unsupportive local culture as a key impediment to execution.*

Park, Seung Ho, Gerardo R. Ungson, and Andrew Cosgrove. *Scaling the Tail: Managing Profitable Growth in Emerging Markets.* New York: Palgrave Macmillan, 2015. DOI: 10.1057/9781137538598.0017.

Execution is the third anchor to profitable growth. As argued earlier, a good strategy is likely to fail without the adequate support of management systems. There are key differences between higher and lower performing firms in regard to their approaches to execution. Higher performing firms are more likely to delegate authority to local management whom they regard as having good ability and competence. Lower performing firms do not consider their local management in the same manner. Higher performing firms see external barriers that limit both demand and supply, which can affect their differentiation strategies. In contrast, lower performing firms view regulation and poor infrastructure in general as barriers. Interestingly, higher performing firms regard an unsupportive local culture as a key impediment to execution.

Decide on what to centralize or decentralize

The locus of decision making has important implications on how well strategies are supported by management structures. The degree of centralization can have differential effects on the extent and form of management control and coordination. Typically, centralized control is consistent with perceived predictability of the environment by headquarters, or particularly relevant to a firm that is seeking to implement a strategy in a uniform fashion. Decentralization is more appropriate when information about local operations cannot be more effectively obtained from headquarters than it can be from the local units. Within multinational firms, control is reflected in the amount of power (decentralization) provided to local units operating in emerging markets.

Establishing the organizational center of gravity is important in emerging economies because markets are granular and uneven in development, requiring different strategic approaches for each sector. In context, decentralization is commonly associated with the requirements of localization because it is becoming increasingly clear that informed local decisions are best suited to recognize and respond to previously nascent consumer preferences and patterns. But how much should be delegated? What should be centralized or retained at the headquarters' level? Should this decision be based on the growth of particular market segments?

In interviews, respondents noted that centralization or delegation depends on whichever functional activity is best suited for local management, and the extent to which benefits from centralization can still be realized. As stated earlier, Godfret Nthunzi, Executive Vice President for Finance, Colgate India, asserts: "You really cannot run a national marketing campaign in India and expect to be successful. You can't assume that the consumer in the north and the other in the south of the country will receive your message in the same way. To deal with this complexity, we have ensured that our marketing group is as diverse as the country is."[1]

Relatedly, Swee Leng Ng, CFO of Mondolez China, argues: "Decisions come from the regions...decisions regarding packaging, flavor, sales models, business models, and decisions about regional distribution centers—all of these decisions are being made locally."[2]

However, there is the risk of overlocalization, prompting the need to balance the requirements of centralization and localization over time. One interviewee stated:

> Procurement has to be global...for the reasons of economies of scale, purchasing power, and negotiating power. Strategic marketing has to be global and local because you have to ensure that everything is in line with the general strategy, but it has to be local as well to be sure that we meet the local needs. Sales organisation is obviously local. Finance has to be both global and local.

In our survey, higher performing firms provide more autonomy to local management in most marketing decisions; in contrast, lower performing firms tend to centralize these activities. This finding reflects more confidence on the part of a higher performing firm to allow more discretion to local units in formulating and implementing marketing and operational activities (Figure 8.1).

Consistent with the previous pattern of findings, local activities in higher performing firms are more decentralized in terms of most functional activities compared to their counterparts in lower performing firms. In lower performing firms, finance and information technology reflect more centralized activities that are more the domain of headquarters. For higher performing firms, they tend to decentralize most other functional activities, notably research and development, sales, marketing, procurement, supply chain, and distribution (Figure 8.2).

94 *Scaling the Tail*

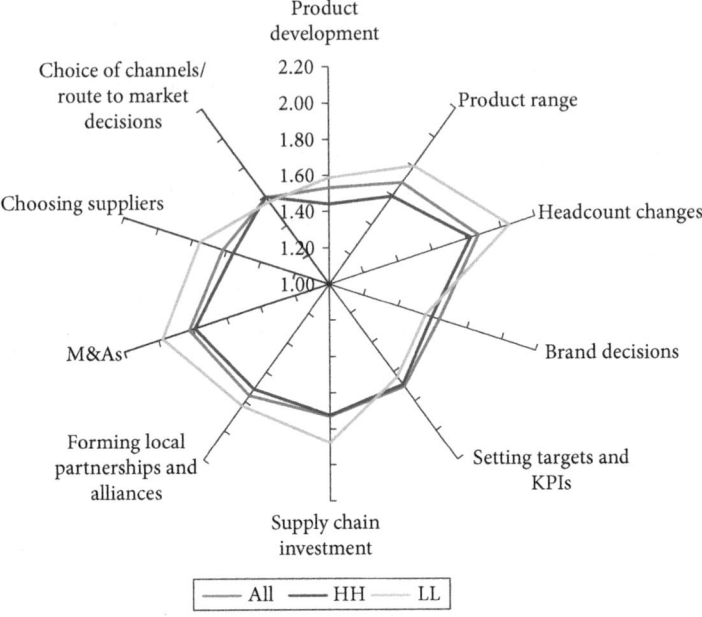

FIGURE 8.1 *The role of local management in business decisions*

The former Southeast Asia leader of a household appliance manufacturer asserts:

> The supply chain has to be global and local, as well, because we want to achieve a global and better organisation in terms of the supply chain. So, it has to be managed by someone at the top level. But, at the same time, we have to take all of the responsibility to be as efficient as possible in terms of the supply chain, forecasts, deliveries, etc. Human resource management obviously has to be local, even if we follow the guidelines of the global strategy. This is particularly true if you manage people here in Asia, especially in Thailand, which I think is the most difficult country in South East Asia in terms of management.

Recognize external barriers to execution

Effective implementation entails a thorough understanding of the obstacles to required actions and strategies. In this study, we explored factors

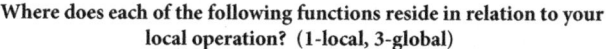

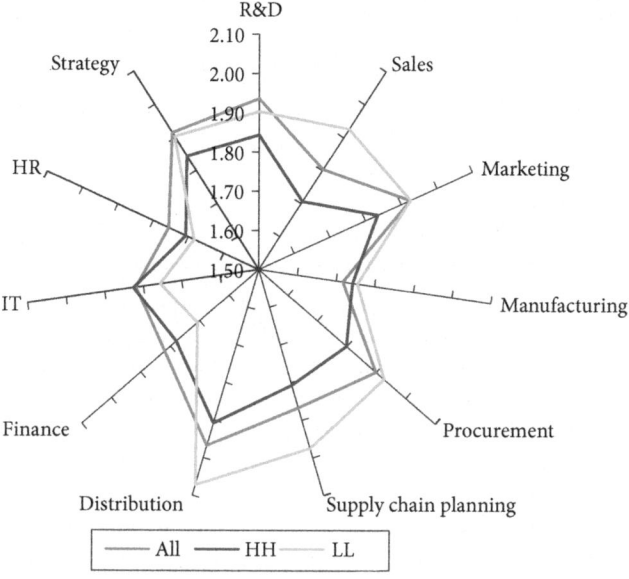

FIGURE 8.2 *The localization of business activities*

that impede the implementation of strategies, whether these reside at the strategic or local levels. Following extensive interviews, our question was: What were external barriers to implementation or execution? In our survey, firms view *labor and input costs, competitive pressure, regulations,* and *market fragmentation* as major external barriers. However, lower performing firms also see poor infrastructure as a key barrier (Figure 8.3).

Rising labor costs can render an erstwhile strategy based on differentiation and cost leadership ineffective. Herbalife took advantage of China's labor costs at the time when the Chinese government had offered incentives for foreign enterprises to invest in the mainland.[3] With rising labor costs on the horizon after a few years, Herbalife initiated the production of raw materials and local herbal supplies, which China has in abundant supply, to offset rising labor costs. Even so, in addition to competitive forays by its key competitor, Amway, Herbalife faces changing regulations concerning direct marketing that pose a risk to its overall operations.

Regulation by way of protectionism presents another possible obstacle, and, as explained by an interviewee in a household appliance company, this can be nuanced:

> First of all, the protectionism exists at different levels. It includes custom duties; so, you have to pay up to a 30% tax for small domestic appliances when they are imported from Europe. Secondly, there is hidden protectionism in terms of a certification process. When the products are made, for example, they must be certified by a government body in Malaysia, Thailand, and Indonesia. This certification process is very tough to pass. Moreover, it will be tougher for European companies.
>
> There is another form of protectionism. It concerns television advertising campaigns. For example, you could produce your complete television campaign and then, when you try to pass the test in Thailand or another country, it is rejected due to censorship. You may be told something like, "You cannot show that, it's too dangerous," etc. Then, one of your television advertisements is no longer 30 seconds, it is reduced to 15 seconds. So, it is very difficult to compete with other brands. This is something that is frequently underestimated, and we have to keep in mind that there is some protectionism here which supports the need of local products, local partnerships, and local manufacturing sites not only in China, but in South East Asia, as well.

The challenge of market fragmentation presents a double-edged sword: it can limit a firm's strategy if consolidation is the intended objective, but it can also open the door for a dual or a multiple segment strategy that is frequently employed by profitable growth firms. Servicing multiple markets partly offset by increased modern trade was brought about principally by the establishment of supermarkets, shopping centers, and hypermarkets. Both offer the potential of consolidating sales in specific urban and rural areas.

One consumer products interviewee explains how modern trade can offer advantages, although the problem of infrastructure remains:

> For international companies, they find modern trade to be more convenient and easier to use to grow their business. European and American companies like department stores because that means the price is higher, it is easy to negotiate in hypermarkets. It is like in France in the 1960s or 1970s, when hypermarkets were growing a lot. It is the case now in Thailand. In Thailand, hypermarkets are very strong. Department stores are popular, as well. But, if you go to Vietnam, it is strictly impossible. There are projects, but infrastructure is not at the right level, the roads are very bad, etc., so it

is difficult to transport your goods. You just have 20 hypermarkets in the country, while the rest is traditional trade and some department stores.

If you want to be sure that you are targeting the middle class market in Indonesia, with 240 million people, then you have to propose products with a margin of 30% maximum. This is why if you go to a store in Indonesia, you will not see so many international brands.

For example, our global brand is very strong in Thailand because it is not an emerging market, but I would say rather an emerged market. It is already emerged. But, if you go to Indonesia, the brand is not so developed because it is very difficult to compete with local brands which are proposing products at average gross margins of 15% to 20%. So, even if you have a very good brand and you propose a 50% margin, you will remain in the niche market.

Be equally aware of internal barriers to implementation

It is widely believed that barriers are not only external; in fact, internal barriers, more commonly thought of as resistance-to-change, can thwart even a well-conceived strategy. Following extensive interviews, we defined internal factors that can impede implementation and execution.

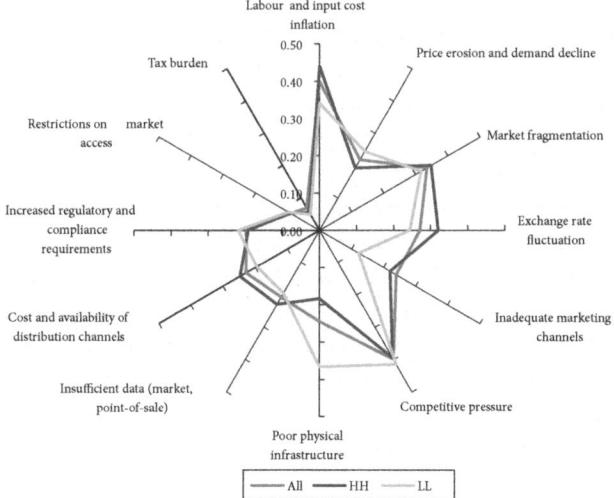

FIGURE 8.3   *External barriers to profitable growth*

Which of the following internal factors do you see as the biggest barriers to your company's profitable growth?

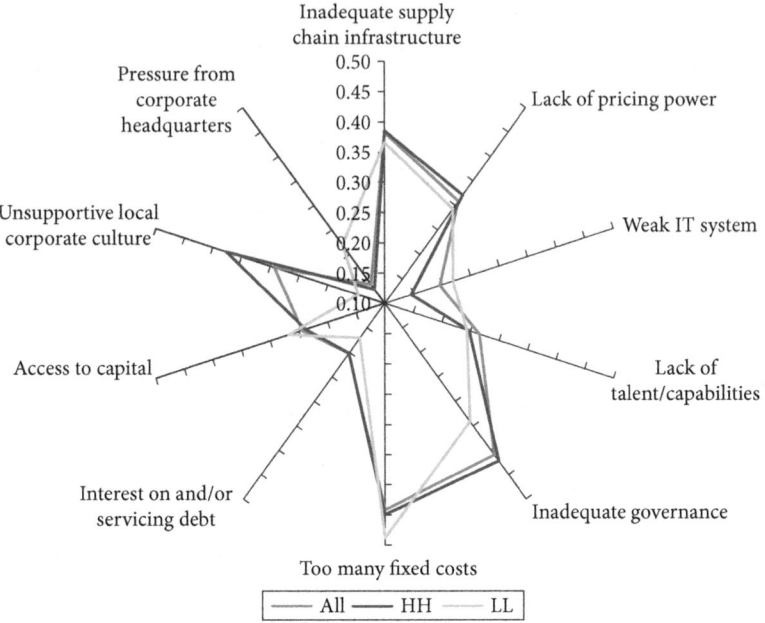

FIGURE 8.4 *Internal barriers to profitable growth*

Our findings indicate that higher performing firms view *unsupportive local cultures, inadequate governance, and inadequate supply chain infrastructure* as primary internal barriers whereas lower performing firms view *fixed costs* and *inadequate supply chain infrastructure* as key internal barriers (Figure 8.4).

An unsupportive local corporate culture and poor governance are underscored in view of the growing importance of local management (more on this later in the section). As indicated, a recurrent theme throughout the study is the importance of localization in all aspects—product, management, and even community relations. In our view, this can make the difference between high and low performing firms in emerging markets.

According to one interviewee,

> If you want to succeed in Asia, it is very difficult to do that from Europe. You must have located teams regarding marketing, and these marketing

teams must have a huge impact on the definition of the products. When I am talking about marketing, I am not talking about trade marketing shuffling about teams to deal with below-the-line investment and how to grow the business in stores. What I am talking about is strategic marketing. This is one of the viable ways European, Western, or international companies can grow their businesses in Asia, which differs so much from country to country.

Invest in local human capital

In this study, a recurring theme was how the very concept of localization needs to evolve. As stated, earlier treatises conceptualized localization as sheer product extensions or refinements to accommodate lower income sectors. In our study of "rough diamonds," localization meant revamping products and product lines to address more sophisticated requirements of fast-growing sectors. In this study, localization has deepened in application to mean significant investment in local talent, rather than simply hiring them.

According to another interviewee, this need arises from a more educated workforce who are closer in terms of knowing the deep preferences of the local community.

> What you have to bear in mind is that the quality of the workers, except in Malaysia maybe, is really appreciated and welcome here. I can see that now in Thailand, which is much higher than Indonesia or China. For cost reasons, the European companies that were in Thailand before the [Asian] crisis are now returning to this region. I think that this is just the beginning of the trend.
>
> It is a good investment [people] because of the hidden costs of key people who have to be trained. But, you train them for nothing if you lose them, at which time the costs are much higher. You have to pay people appropriately... you have to invest in communication.

Take the case of Ajinomoto we interviewed.[4] As a Japanese company, the firm adheres to its cultural tradition of nurturing local talent, with the expectation that extremely loyal personnel will be produced and that retention rates would be higher. Even when people do leave, Ajinomoto takes pride in that the departed often retain very positive feelings toward the company.

Learning about local circumstances is a critical component of Unilever (Malaysia) Holdings SdnBhd's successful brand localization strategy. In an interview, it was disclosed:

> Good adaptability to the local market is one of the main factors that contributed to the success of Unilever. Unilever is always able to find the opportunity to shift from an international brand to a local brand that natives are willing to accept. For example, Unilever (Malaysia) Holdings SdnBhd embarked on a "Malaysian Favourites" Campaign at all Tesco stores nationwide between 29 July 2009 and 26 August 2009 in line with its "Vitality" mission of doing good for the community. In addition, Unilever (Malaysia) Holdings SdnBhd has also acquired several local companies and signed agreements with a local celebrity to promote its brands.

Localization decisions are not confined to augmentations or enhancements in products or services to cater to local tastes. Such decisions extend to the management of local teams, or employees that are drawn from the local market. Similar to local versus global issues relating to product adaptation, strategies to build a local management team can determine a firm's ability to execute its primary strategy of differentiation. Overlocalization can lead to cost inefficiency and workplace redundancy whereas underlocalization can lead to a dysfunctional dependence on central headquarters. As in most management decisions, an optimal balance is needed.

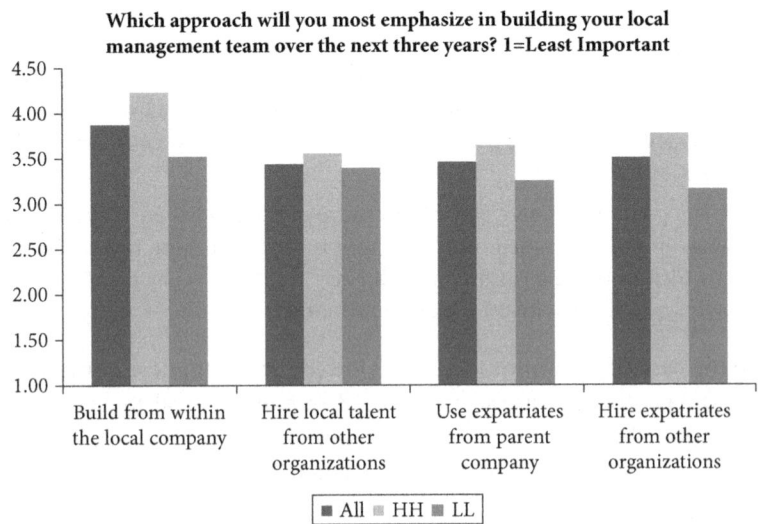

FIGURE 8.5 *Strategies for building local management teams*

A Southeast Asia consumer products leader EY interviewed believes:

> You must dedicate local strategic marketing teams. I do not believe any more in centralised marketing or strategic marketing departments. Of course, for the vice presidents, why not? But, if these teams stay at headquarters, they cannot understand the market. The impact then on products is huge, and the products are not adapted well. So, you must dedicate strategic marketing teams to the local markets. I am not saying that you need strategic teams all over the world or in 150 countries. But, obviously, for South East Asia, you must have a dedicated team for this region. You also need one for Northeast Asia, Japan and Korea, which are very different markets, very different from Southeast Asia. Even in Southeast Asia, there are major differences between Singapore, which is a mature market, and Indonesia, which is a very modern market.
>
> I think the local responsibilities and the local design of the products are critically important if you want to succeed in these countries. If you want to do it on your own and not do any partnership with local players, then you have to adapt your product drastically. You must live in the particular country or you must be close to the markets to develop and design the right products. If you cannot do that, then think about a partnership to use local talents and local products.

In our study, higher performing firms build from within and hire local talent from others, but also rely on hiring expatriates for special circumstances whereas lower performing firms focus on using expatriates from other organizations and from their parent companies (Figure 8.5). In the case of Cadbury-India, the management team consists of local Indian employees who are dedicated to local needs. This structure has led to changing the chocolate formula in ways that prevent melting in the country's hot weather. In fact, packaging and marketing decisions are all made locally. This emphasis on building local capabilities defines higher performance. Moreover, higher performing firms differ significantly from lower performing firms in terms of their perceptions of the effectiveness of their local teams, with the higher performing firms reporting significantly higher confidence.

Create a performance-based corporate culture

Taken altogether, strategies, processes, and structures have to co-align in order for profitable growth to ensue. Otherwise, there will be mismatches, inconsistency, and even disruption. One way of achieving this unity is through strong and supportive management systems that are linked closely to the requirements of a given strategy and that offer incentives to ensure consistency over time. The key to success is the ability of the company to predict and control important environmental events that then provide core inputs into the strategy and management structures. In our survey, we investigated the ability of higher and lower performers to assess their environments (Figure 8.6).

Our findings underscore the importance of a proactive approach to assessment. Specifically, higher performers endeavor to predict their environments as much as possible, employ formal planning systems, develop managers who are comfortable with change and flexibility, and prepare for worst-case contingencies. In contrast, lower performing firms report greater difficulty at predictions, with limited planning systems, tighter control of local managers, and relying on cost control to account for unpredictable environments.

Because implementation is a broad and complex process, respondents referred to specific aspects of management systems that are supportive of the general strategy. The chief customer officer of a global personal care company discusses the importance of creating corporate cultures based on supportive systems: "We are trying to build a whole culture

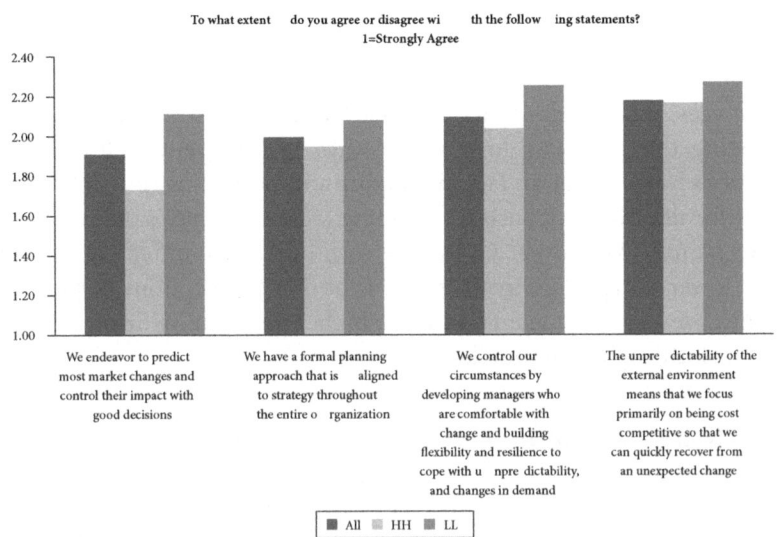

FIGURE 8.6 *Developing local strategic capabilities*

of celebrating in-store execution, which we believe is one of the three factors that is going to drive business globally."

In a specific context, a Japanese food company interviewee expresses the need for delegation at the local level:

> While authority continues to shift to local operations, governance remains firmly with the head office. It is based on the belief that the core of the company's business is local. We leave decisions in local hands whenever possible. The head office business department's role is to thoroughly support local operations, prevent sub-optimization, and ensure that all employees are heading in the same direction. The most recent example of the continuing shift of authority to local offices is the shift of new product development authority to local offices.

Moreover, he states:

> For new product development, we previously conducted the *"ringi"* process (process of circular memo) for approval at our head office in Japan. However, to increase decision-making speed, we are in the process of delegating such authority to local offices. Offices in ASEAN regions already basically rely on local discretion, and we are planning to apply this same process in other regions.

Colgate Palmolive India, Ltd., developed an in-house talent structure to identify, nurture, and incentivize critical human resource placements in marketing, sales, and consumer marketing. It is noted that close to 10% of these employees receive international training over a five-year period. The company likewise invests in resilient information technology to facilitate the exchange of financial information and other data relating to operational efficiency.[5] Similarly, Hindustan Unilever has developed dedicated human resource managers that are focused on particular businesses. Nestle India, Ltd., employs an open decision-making environment and delegates key decisions to local units. Specifically, the company created separate business units (strategic business units) to address the emerging requirements of modern trade.[6] PepsiCo empowered two divisions to make decisions (Himalayan Market Unit and Peninsular Market Unit) to respond more quickly to its environment.[7]

A senior manager in Hindustan Unilever India indicates that management development is rooted in good decisions based on reliable information:

> Managing the flow of information is one of the main tasks that a company needs to focus on. Companies are required to deal with a huge amount of

internal and external information every day, and efficient management of information is a prerequisite for managers to make optimal high-level decisions and achieve business objectives. One of the ways that we have [to] dealt with this challenge is by establishing a knowledge base called the "knowledge workshop." It includes many areas of knowledge and is equipped with experts from various fields... For example, the detergent business spans multiple segments in response to previous nascent sectors, including premium (Surf and Ariel), mid-price (Rin, Henko, Tide), and popular segments (Ghari, Wheel, Nirma, Mr. White). What is impressive is that these brands account for 15%, 40%, and 45% of the market share, respectively, or 60% of the total market. The remaining 40% is taken by regional and small unorganized players... researchers and salespeople are enabled to communicate through the system, and thus respond quickly to market changes.

Anthony Tsai (introduced earlier), also added: "In the past, it was enough to send in a person from the main headquarters. Then, the attention was focused on hiring local talent. But, this too is no longer enough. The key to future success is not sheer delegation, but training and developing capabilities at the local level.

In the soaring healthcare sector, specifically, Herbalife China decided to hire and train local managers for key positions, in contrast to Amway's approach of bringing in outside managers (e.g., an executive from Hong Kong).[8] In India, Unilever's cultivation of the "Shakti" system, now approaching 50,000 in number, involves the use of local women to directly sell its products in remote places that would otherwise be inaccessible through conventional channels.[9] As the pioneer in Indonesia's palm oil industry, PT Cahaya Kalbar Tbk, has achieved great success in capitalizing on raw materials and forging distribution channels based on its deep knowledge of the local population.[10] Yamaha (Thailand) Company, Ltd., adopts flexible work arrangements and value-based management that align local operations with corporate objectives.[11]

Kraft Malaysia has a distinguished management system that bridges personnel training, incentives, and raw materials management.[12] The company focuses on and recruits university graduates who are individually trained for specific company operations. Training is given for subjects including business, leadership, and functional disciplines. Senior management comes from different cultural backgrounds, including talented managers from multinationals and related industries. The company established an "Innovation Award" designed to encourage employees to think outside of the box. Finally, given the importance of raw materials in the company's food and beverage portfolio, it also possesses a special program dedicated to raw material management.

In all, the benefits of a performance-based culture are summed up well by one Southeast Asia consumer products leader:

> People are very interested in joining an international company to be sure that they will be more respected and better treated. This is critically important in the local context. Local people are quite proud to be able to fix issues themselves, as well. They are not waiting for the help of others, and are very proud of that fact. They are not waiting for the company to invest in a local network. What is important is to choose the right people and have them participate in the growth. It is, thus, essential to invest some money and to acquire good people.
>
> We have not come here just to bring in Western or expatriate talent, but rather to also invest and recruit local people, and to give them a good job with a good salary. We also show a high level of respect for the local people, and this is so important in the eyes of Asian people, in general. The company is considered to be a second family, so the way that you behave is very critical. There are no trade unions, and they do not need them here. But, the way that you treat and respect them is really appreciated. So, it is a way to participate in the growth of a country and the success of the region.
>
> As long as you are informed, or willing to be informed and learn about the country and the region, and as long as you are patient and can wait for three to five years, you can have a very good return on investment. But, it does require some investment, some patience, and some adaptation in the areas of management and products. Then, everything is possible.

Summing up—co-aligning strategies with management structures and processes

There are noticeable differences between high and low performing firms in terms of execution capabilities and localization approaches. High performing firms internally develop and nurture capable local management teams and systems. They tend to decentralize key functional activities and business decisions that are supported by a strong performance-oriented culture. The empowered local management is better able to sense and address local consumer needs, anticipate and respond to market volatility, and take proactive approaches in strategic decisions than low performing firms (see Figure 8.7). Low performing firms fail

106 Scaling the Tail

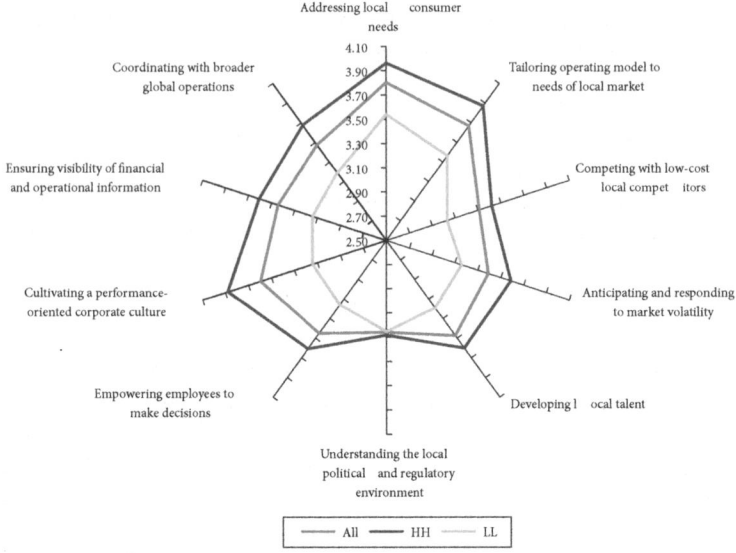

FIGURE 8.7 *Effectiveness of the local management team*

to develop confident local management teams and rely on a centralized control system to manage local operations. There is thus little motivation to cultivate a performance-oriented culture and decentralize key functional activities in poor-performing firms. There are also stark contrasts between high and low performing firms regarding their perceptions of external and internal challenges. Given their active involvement in local operations, high performing firms pay closer attention to challenges in the task environment, such as cost factors and market structure, and the soft elements of management, such as culture and governance. On the contrary, low performing firms see challenges in the broad macro environment, such as regulation and infrastructure, and the hard elements of the management, such as IT infrastructure and capital. In sum, it is essential to follow an appropriate localization strategy to successfully execute profitable growth strategies in emerging markets. In the new competitive environment, localization needs to extend beyond simple product extensions and refinements; it requires a major investment in developing local talent along with granular approaches to refine market positioning and product lines in local markets (Table 8.1).

TABLE 8.1 *Differentiating higher and lower performing firms in co-alignment*

Survey item	Higher performer (HH)	Lower performer (LL)
Locus of control	Decentralized	Centralized
External barriers to execution	Cost inflation; market fragmentation	Increased regulation; poor infrastructure
Internal barriers to execution	Unsupportive local culture; inadequate governance	Weak IT infrastructure; access to capital
Conceptions of control	Greater ability to control for unpredictable events	Moderate ability to control for unpredictable events
Local management and competence	Highly competent local management	Weak local managerial capabilities
Building a profit-oriented culture	Point of emphasis	Desired, but not as essential
Localization focus	Nurturing local talent; flexible market adaptation	Headcount; product range; supplier management

Notes

1. EY. "Profit-or-lose. Balancing the growth-profit paradox for global consumer products companies and retailers in Asia's emerging markets." 2013. http://emergingmarkets.ey.com/profit-or-lose-2/.
2. Ibid.
3. See http://www.herbalife.cn http://www.chinadaily.com.cn/english/doc/2005-01/27/content_412659.htm; http://www.zjtrchem.com/eshownews.asp?id=77; http://sports.cqnews.net/html/2011-05/17/content_6364361.htm; http://www.amway.com.cn.
4. Interview took place on March 27, 2013. Interviewee requested anonymity.
5. See http://www.fundinguniverse.com/company-histories/colgate-palmolive-company histories.
6. http://archive.financialexpress.com/news/why-nestle-india-does-not-want-a-revolution/83600/0.
7. http://en.wikipedia.org/wiki/PepsiCo.
8. http://www.fortunechina.com/management/c/2011-05/31/content_58181.htm.
9. http://www.hul.co.in/sustainable-living-2014/casestudies/Casecategory/Project-Shakti.aspx.
10. http://www.wilmarcahayaindonesia.com/.
11. For reference, see http://www.yamaha.com/about_yamaha/ir/presentation/pdf-data/2013/pres-130405e.pdf.
12. See http://baike.baidu.com/view/4199561.htm?fromId=266828#2 and http://www.coca-colacompany.com/

9
A Synthesis of Our Findings

Abstract: *Our objective is to examine the dynamics of profitable growth in emerging markets. Collectively, our findings are as follows: First, growth and profitability can be viewed as interspersed in sequential stages. Firms might initially focus on profits or growth, and would purposefully seek a balance of optimal states in the future. Second, the dynamics, however, are tempered by significant changes in the external environment. Third, while emerging markets are generally viewed as fast growing, growth is not uniform, but granular. Not all local markets are the same, nor do they respond to foreign multinational products and services in the same way. Specific pockets of demand develop quicker from their nascent states than others. Understanding the dynamics of scale for different market segments is the critical strategy.*

Park, Seung Ho, Gerardo R. Ungson, and Andrew Cosgrove. *Scaling the Tail: Managing Profitable Growth in Emerging Markets.* New York: Palgrave Macmillan, 2015. DOI: 10.1057/9781137538598.0018.

A Synthesis of Our Findings 109

Taken collectively, this study reaffirms the difficulty of tracking enduring patterns in the midst of change, transitions, and evolution. There is unanimity among academic scholars that the core objective of strategy is to attain a sustainable competitive advantage. When the proverbial rubber meets the road, however, what emerges is that few, if any, firms are able to sustain advantage for long, and that competitive skills and capabilities can be fleeting in light of changing circumstances.

Accordingly, our focus in this study constituted a less onerous track, that is, to examine the dynamics of profitable growth. Growth and profitability can be viewed as interspersed in sequential stages. Firms might initially focus on profits or growth and would purposefully seek a balance of optimal states in the future. The dynamics, however, are tempered by significant changes in the external environment. While emerging markets are generally viewed as fast growing, or approximately 3.2% more than developed economies, growth is not uniform, but granular. Not all local markets are the same, nor do they respond to foreign multinational products and services in the same way. Specific pockets of demand develop more rapidly from their nascent states than others.

Capitalizing on granular growth

Unlike previously, emerging markets are much more pronounced with granular growth or uneven development across regions and cities, most notably the growth arising from affluent middle-class sectors that form propitious market niches. On the surface, popular conceptions of any middle class tend to emphasize their affluence and propensity for consumption. In this study, however, global managers reported that the proclivities of middle-class sectors in emerging markets differ markedly from their counterparts in developed countries. Because the middle class, particularly in China and India, is a fledgling sector with attendant nuances and insecurities, foreign multinationals and emerging local enterprises alike have to develop new skills and capabilities in order for profitable growth to ensue.

Such skills and capabilities are captured in what respondents referred to as developing multi-branding in different product categories to accommodate broader, if not conflicting, demand preferences by the middle class in emerging markets. In context, the emphasis shifts from scaling based on products to scaling based on product categories, hence leading to our formulation of "scaling of the tail" as a major strategy of value-creation.

Scaling the tail—responding to granular growth

In our formulation, scaling the tail combines the features of two earlier sources of value: "straddling the tail" and the "long tail." Unlike the former, scaling the tail is not centered on maturing mass merchandising products for which extensions are needed to extend product maturity. On the contrary, it is not simply a replication of the long tail, in that scaling is possible and imminent in fast-developing, previously difficult-to-reach, market sectors located at the tail. What further differentiates it from the long tail is the centrality of agglomeration as the driving force in aggregation. The long tail has no such agglomeration effects, that is, sales tend to be atomistic and episodic, although increasing large in cumulative numbers.

Scaling the tail challenges traditional concepts of entry strategies and provides one explanation for why the traditional reliance of scaling based on mass merchandising alone fails. The logic of mass merchandising follows that of mass manufacturing, in which scale and scope economies arise from repeated use or purchase of the commodity product. However, it does not apply when the industry is not a commodity and when branding is consequential to strategy.

Traditional versus emerging mindsets

Collectively, the changing phases of competition accentuate the main differences between traditional and conventional strategic mindsets and introduce an emerging transformative orientation based on strategic positioning, capitalizing on competitive drivers, and building supportive management systems. To illustrate this further, Table 9.1 reproduces the first part of our analysis (see Table 3.1) with specific strategies that reflect new thinking based on the findings.

The "P-E-C" diagnostic framework

As indicated, our initial interviews centered on successful firms that followed a differentiated strategy, with an emphasis on high-impact

TABLE 9.1 *Conventional entry strategies versus emerging strategic templates**

Conventional entry strategy	Emerging strategic templates
Enter mass consumption markets, primarily commodities, in which unit costs can be scaled up through manufacturing and distribution	Enter nascent, fragmented markets that have significant potential for high-end brand development
Recalibrate existing products in order to reduce costs and to make them affordable	Set prices high or commensurate to recovering fixed and variable costs; develop a portfolio of brands for high-return segments
When appropriate, localize features of the product or service to meet the local needs and expectations	Localization is a requirement, not a luxury; intensive consumer behavior research should underpin decision to localize
Employ expats as experts and hire local talent	Hiring local talent is a necessary, but not sufficient, requirement for success; successful and aspiring firms have to invest in training local talent
Construct supply chains that link the different manufacturing units to select markets	Supply chains are needed, but investment should focus on virtual linkages and processes, not necessarily on physical infrastructure

Note: * As indicated, the narrative on conventional strategy is adopted from S. Shankar, C. Ormiston, N. Bloch, R. Schaus, & V. Vishwanath, "How to win in emerging markets," *MIT Sloan Management Review*, 49(3):18–24. Product No. 49309, 2008.

branding. Hence, we were interested in the extent to which scaling the tail effects were manifest across firms from emerging markets that varied with respect to performance. Moreover, we were interested in the manner in which branding was applied, and how this might have an impact on profitable growth. In particular, we wanted to discern enduring patterns across three major categories: (1) positioning; (2) exploring key drivers for success; and (3) co-aligning with management systems.

Our findings that are presented in the previous three chapters reveal a specific pattern: all firms, whether these were classified as higher or lower performers, pursued a product differentiation strategy. What distinguished high and low performance was the firms' abilities and capabilities in executing this differentiation strategy. The survey results corroborate the employment of strong multi-brands with multiple segmentation strategies to capture the resurging middle class or related pockets of affluence. Taken collectively, the findings punctuate drivers for attaining profitable growth over time. Specific findings are highlighted in Table 9.2.

TABLE 9.2 *The P-E-C diagnostic framework and strategic drivers*

The P-E-C diagnostic framework	Strategic drivers
P—Positioning for profitable growth	Selection of strong brands Multiple segmentation strategies Flanking the segments with a portfolio of strong brands Intensive consumer behavior research
E—Exploring key drivers for success	Marketing strategy (price points; branding; and enhancing distribution channels) Localization strategy (consumer behavior research to encompass demographic, behavioral, and psychographic interests) Opportunities to differentiate (intensive marketing through investment in data centers) and cost control (centralization of key functions)
C—Co-alignment with management systems	Building a performance-based culture (local autonomy; balancing centralization/decentralization; distribution; R & D; and procurement) Addressing external and internal barriers Hiring and training local talent
Summary: How winning firms "scale the tail"	The strategy is to explore opportunities for product differentiation, without sacrificing costs. The logic is to select high-end brands; assess their demand across different segments; agglomerate common tendencies; utilize multiple drivers; and create a highly responsive performance-based culture

To revisit our earlier formulations, how do our findings depict the logic of "scaling the tail"? In Figure 9.1, the first half of the exhibit replicates an earlier one that depicts value-creation in "scaling the tail" based on interviews. Combining these findings with those from the survey, the second half illustrates the differences between firms of varying levels of performance.

Not unlike most empirical studies, there are limitations that principally arise from what we decided to include and exclude. Our focus was on the consumer goods and retailing industry, with particular attention paid to the growth of the middle-class sector in emerging markets. Accordingly, our findings and conclusions stem largely from multinationals pursuing a differentiation strategy in response to these growth sectors. However, because we did not examine other income sectors, our study does not rule out the employment of cost leadership

A Synthesis of Our Findings 113

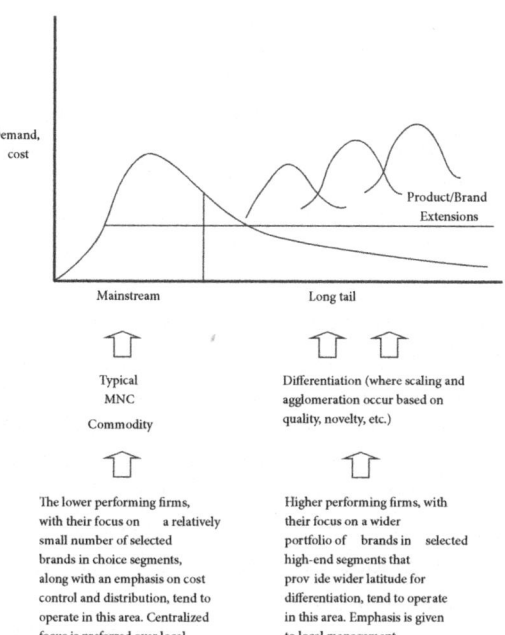

FIGURE 9.1 *The logic of "scaling the tail"*

strategies aimed at building scale. The traditional entry strategy might still be effective for multinationals targeting lower-income sectors with a standard commodity product. Our argument is that the application of the manufacturing logic to a merchandising one is not universalistic and needs to be thought out more thoroughly when applied to other contexts and industries. Changing competitive landscapes have brought new imperatives, as vividly expressed by Ehab Oaf, whose extensive interview with us is the feature in Box 9.1. Can these findings be blended in ways to provide specific prescriptions for multinational firms? The final chapter addresses this question.

BOX 9.1 *An interview with Ehab Abou Oaf*

> *An Interview with Ehab Abou Oaf, Asia-Pacific president of Mars Chocolate, a world-renowned manufacturer of chocolate bars and products. In this brief, he provides his ideas on profitable growth and other ideas discussed in the book.*

Growth in developed and emerging markets

Set realistic expectations. When thinking about an emerging market, you do not necessarily set the same level of expectations for profitable growth as you would do for developed markets. Specifically, expectations should be in line with growth potential. Like in developed markets, we are concerned about profitable growth, but emerging markets will have different time horizons and expectations.

Understand the dynamics of scaling. Develop a good understanding of scale or the dynamics of growth. In China, for example, which has achieved scale to a degree, you would expect profitable growth, although not necessarily the same level of profits as you would expect from a more developed market. In contrast, for markets like Indonesia or the Philippines, they are still relatively nascent in the development stage. In effect, you need to reset and balance expectations not only between the developed and the developing markets, but even within developing and emerging markets.

Know how scale can affect growth and profitability. Understanding the dynamics of scaling is, hence, essential to your goals for the market. If your goal is profitability, but if this cannot be supported by scale in the long run, this goal is not sustainable, even with short-term profits. Moreover, competitive pressure and other disruptive forces can easily disrupt your strategy.

Requirements to succeed

Relate scaling to brand strategy. Understanding the elements of scaling that generate growth is the first requirement. Take the case of China, where you might have more than one brand, with others in various stages of development. There are the big or power brands, which have a substantial size to drive profitability. But at the same time, there are newer brands that you anticipate will lead to larger scale in the future. Both sets of brands require different skill-sets and understanding, whose differences are critical.

Focus on critical areas. In any given market potential, it is tempting to pursue a broad strategy that entails multiple directions, additional investments, and resources. Nevertheless, resources are scarce, and such a broad strategy can cost more money and require attention. Hence, you really need to have a laser-sharp focus on the areas that you will go after, where your profit pools and your targeted investment areas are.

Understand what ensures productivity. Let us dispel any prevailing assumptions. First, cheap labor is the chief means to deliver profitable growth in emerging markets. This assumption is fast eroding, specifically in a market like China. Second, high growth that is principally driven by low productivity is a misleading indicator. Eventually, you will need to keep a very close eye on your overhead and tracking levels of growth to learn what will drive productivity not only in the short run, but in the longer horizon, as well.

Be attentive to new market segments. The fourth requirement is recognition of a growing pool of middle-class consumers that are very affluent. Given this shift, you have to track the potential of this profit pool and develop strategies to service them. Any business model should rely on volume and growth over time, not simply margins in the short run. To succeed, you need a disciplined approach to considering this segment.

Drivers of profitable growth

Understand your targeted segment thoroughly. You need to be clear about your consumer segmentation. Where are the trends? Try to stay ahead of the trends in Asia, for example. Being very familiar with this part of the world, the affluent part of society, such as the middle class, is trending even stronger and faster, and more so than in the developed world. In China, they are making significant leaps, from television to e-commerce, and to assorted social media. E-commerce in China is bigger than in the United States in several segments.

Be agile. Recognize the trends and consumer segmentation that allow you to identify niches, both manifest and nascent. Integrate these findings with your core competences. Certain consumer preferences in China, such as chocolate gifting, are fast becoming a habitual practice. This is an area of profitable growth because this is a high-end segment. People are willing to spend because it is now a part of accepted practice, and it has become an important ritual. In short, tap into consumer habits, insights, and trends. It is critical to identify these niches and go after them with disciplined actions.

Build brands and scale up propositions. In terms of goals, decide on which brands should be profitable. Certain investments every year are needed to support them, and that investment might not necessarily be directly proportional to size. Moreover, you need to determine how long it would take for the brands to achieve the desired level of scale. Be prepared to scale up product categories.

Target the affluent middle class. In emerging markets, you might have to ladder your brands in anticipation of growing affluent middle-class segments. With growing affluence, consumers tend to migrate to higher level, differentiated brands. By laddering brands, you are able to examine the price points and study how various groups change preferences about brands and products as they increase their purchasing power.

Develop a portfolio mindset. When appraising the potential of different emerging markets, adopt a mindset that involves looking at a portfolio of markets. By this, I mean the stages of development and opportunity versus investment. In China, which has massive opportunities, there is the potential for large scale. Similarly, in other developed markets in Asia, such as in Japan and Korea, there are differences in market potential. Other countries might not grow as much, but they can generate the funds that would allow and support investment in other places.

On supportive management systems

Develop a process to support strategies. After knowing the drivers and strategies to attain profitable growth, you will need a systemic plan to implement strategies. You will need to define: where are the gaps, where are the opportunities, where are your financial targets? Part of the management decision cycle is to know which decisions are handled by top management or the local levels. Decisions cover what operations to activate, what investment will breach the gap or capitalize on the opportunities, and decisions that can accelerate growth even further. As a part of the process, you have to close the loop by integrating ideas, forecasts, supply planning, gaps and opportunities, and analysis that gets presented to management and then that goes back to appropriate levels in order to achieve financial targets.

Bring discipline into the process. Without discipline, you will not have profitable growth. A number of companies underpin a discipline with well-designed processes. Such processes bring together entire supply chains with demand-planning cycles. As part of a disciplined process, marketing, sales, and production are able to operate on the same basis, starting with forecasts, to production, to supply chains, and to deliverables.

Build capabilities. Other supporting elements include the need to build capabilities. These involve training and coaching the senior leaders within the local units and providing them with the right support in terms of functional guidance and strategic global initiatives. As a general rule, focus on the local levels, so that you do not lose the line of sight.

Foster a culture of engagement. In building capabilities, you have to create a culture of engagement. First, people have to be clear on what is required of them at every level, from the factory operation level to the general manager level. Second, they also need to have the tools and equipment to do what is expected of their every role. This is not confined to physical elements, but also mental requirements. In all, everyone should be clear on why the decisions are being made and how these are being communicated. Once the objectives are clear, the organization should have appropriate recognition and rewards systems in place to ensure that it cares for individuals.

Set examples through thoughtful execution. Without such a system, you are not going to achieve engagement. With clarity, people know their career progressions, and their expectations of themselves and for others. Setting good examples is critical here. People need to see and believe that their senior management is "walking the talk" in important decisions. Although it is true that not every organization can excel in every aspect, it is important for the organization to focus on three to four standards every year to maintain focus, momentum, and credibility. In all, you will need an "eco-system" in place in order to integrate all of the elements necessary to achieve profitable growth.

Hiring and retaining the best people

Know why people join and stay in organizations. This is the billion dollar question, and there is no straightforward answer to it. In my experience, there are a couple of things that you need to be successful. First, people like to join and stay with successful companies. That is the No.1 rule in my book. People want to be proud. They want to be part of a successful organization. You have to celebrate success because that is what attracts talented people.

Combine talent with engagement. If you do have highly engaged people, they should be likewise clear on what the goals are, that they have the tools, that they are getting recognized, that they're clear on the career path, and that the job is meaningful. If so, you will have a high level of retention.

Define your value proposition. Third, if you want to have an engaging culture, you need to be very clear on the value proposition. For example, in Mars, we pride ourselves in being a privately held company, which means that we will take care of our people based on the long-term rather than looking only at short-term results. We also try to minimize the politics within the organization. On top of that, we are a highly decentralized organization. So, our headquarters is very small. Our regional team consists of 6 or 7 people who manage the entire Asia-Pacific region, for which there are 5,000–6,000 associates.

Major challenges and barriers to execution

Challenge 1: Balancing localization with globalization. One challenge is to balance localization with the infusion of expatriates, and then carefully define the role of regional teams. Typically, a regional team needs to supervise the local team, and more importantly, to train, coach, guide, and function as a sounding board for them. This is critical to ensure the success of that process.

Challenge 2: Getting larger is not necessarily the roadmap to success. As organizations get bigger, coordination becomes much more difficult. Therefore, it becomes important that you have a system in place in which supervision, training, coaching, and other elements are ingrained into the culture. It is also important that this system not be regarded as an enforced behavior from a small subset of individuals.

Challenge 3: Recognize adversity and be prepared to persevere. Admittedly, this is more complicated than it sounds, and I do not wish to convey that these challenges are easy. Creating a performance culture is hard work, and it is not easy to get it right. Managing an organization will always be a work-in-progress. There is no end date to that. So, I hope that I am not misleading you by making it sound like things will necessarily work out. You just get out there and execute.

Note: The IEMS Research Team conducted two interviews with Mr. Oaf (June 9, 2014; March 8, 2013). The transcripts were edited for length, and several sentences were rephrased for continuity.

10
Recommendations

Abstract: *This chapter presents our recommendations for multinational corporations operating in emerging markets with implications for profitable growth: (1) focus on product categories; (2) distinguish between the traditional emphasis on mass consumption based on logic of manufacturing cost strategy to marketing and merchandising that is based on the logic of differentiation; (3) do not interpret localization narrowly as product refinements; it is a learning process that incorporates product adaptation, attention to nascent preferences of a targeted segment, and a proactive approach to developing local talent; (4) go beyond the traditional belief of simply hiring locals. Successful firms train and develop them; and (5) to manage profitable growth in the future, develop a systemic strategy for identifying growth segments and exploring opportunities for "scaling the tail."*

Park, Seung Ho, Gerardo R. Ungson, and Andrew Cosgrove. *Scaling the Tail: Managing Profitable Growth in Emerging Markets.* New York: Palgrave Macmillan, 2015. DOI: 10.1057/9781137538598.0019.

On the whole, what have we learned about profitable growth? How should firms compete in the fast-changing environment of emerging markets? What is the best approach for sustaining high profitability and high sales growth over time? What differentiates firms with varying levels of performance in this process? What are the requirements for "scaling the tail"? This chapter highlights our recommendations for MNCs with implications for strategic practice.

Focus on product categories, or the similarities between product brand and extensions for the fast-developing middle class situated across countries or within a specific region of a given country

This research draws attention to enduring patterns that are common across different emerging markets. While focusing attention on different markets that had varying growth rates that worked well in the past, the development of a burgeoning middle class in these countries has created a propitious segment. The demographics describing this new middle class are as informative as they are revealing. In the case of China, estimates for its emerging middle class range from 100 to 247 million, with similar growth patterns materializing in India, Russia, and Brazil.[1] The rise of the middle class affords new opportunities for growth and development.

Yet, it is no longer the case of selecting an entire country and then capitalizing on its potential, although this comprises a relatively simple entry strategy. Changes in the competitive landscape mandate a new strategy. In order to build scale, it is better to focus on product categories. Specifically, identify a product space, typically the area for differentiated power brands, across different countries or in geographical regions with similar demand patterns in a specific country, and then grow from this vantage point. As noted in our findings, profitable growth firms are more likely to engage in multiple product categories than less profitable growth firms.

This recommendation accords with earlier studies that highlight the importance of specific Tier I (major) and II (secondary) markets. This contrasts with treating one country as a single homogeneous market. As noted earlier, this approach lends itself to growth that is less linear and more "granular." In academic parlance, the primary focus is on differentiating the power brands, growing a targeted segment, and developing a competitive position that can be defended.

In the same vein, distinguish between the traditional emphasis on mass consumption based on the logic of manufacturing cost strategy and marketing and merchandising that is based on the logic of differentiation

Manufacturing and marketing comprise two different logics; the former relates to changes in supply, notably the need to lower costs and improve operational efficiency, while the latter is concerned with changes in the demand curve, particularly shifts in consumer demand, consumption patterns, and income levels. While interdependent, their effectiveness depends on the primacy of a firm's strategy. For example, for sourcing purposes alone, emerging markets were once regarded as a popular site for low-cost operations. Again, the changing landscape impels the need for reassessing this strategy.

As detailed in this report, targeting new consumer markets inhabits a completely different logic. Cultural differences impel new preferences and expectations. Numerous interviewees expressed the dissimilarity of consumers from more traditional beliefs. Consumers in emerging markets are described as "complex" and "insecure," and in need of "multi-touch" attention. For this reason, most respondents called for the need to invest heavily in marketing research and data infrastructure to obtain deep knowledge of this segment. Moreover, more traditional concepts, such as relational capital, while manifest in these countries as a whole, might not be as compelling or as pervasive as before. Hence, competency-based knowledge emerges as a new requirement for success.

Although the need for differentiated products was explicit in the interviews, survey findings disclose that there are different drivers to gain advantages from a differentiation strategy. There is a significant variation in the selection of drivers; higher performing firms tend to select price, quality, price points, and brand strength. Differentiation allows firms to charge a higher price point to improve margins. Thus, firms are more conscious of seeking opportunities for extending differentiation advantages. Correspondingly, investments to enhance visibility and market presence are seen to be the key to future success in the consumer goods sector. In retailing, it is online sales, reflecting the growing popularity of this channel. However, there are differences in terms of dependency on capital resources. High performance firms are more likely to view the importance of shared resources (i.e., balanced centralized/decentralized) between headquarters and local units, compared to lower performing firms that principally depend on headquarters for financial support and strategic advice.

Localization should not be interpreted narrowly as product refinements; it is a learning process that incorporates product adaptation, attention to nascent preferences of a targeted segment, and a proactive approach to developing local talent

Localization is a phrase in good currency. It is touted as the preferred alternative to the assignment of expatriates, a process that can be expensive. In our study, we found widespread support for localization, particularly as observed from the experiences of higher performing firms. Nevertheless, localization is not a panacea, as an extreme form of localization can bring about significantly high costs and eventual inefficiency. Moreover, there is the risk that local talent might not be an adequate replacement for the deep experience possessed by seasoned international expatriates.[2]

Accordingly, three findings add nuance to this localization. First, localization is not a single episodic event or decision, but a process that permeates the adaptation process. Second, localization is not simply proclaimed, but entails an intensive study of underlying cultural patterns.[3] Third, localization is multifaceted, which entails deep decentralization in decision making, such as in the support for local brand propositions, leveraging local R & D, and marketing decisions. In fact, one consistent finding from the surveys is that higher performing firms are more likely to delegate key responsibilities to their local counterparts than are lower performing firms.

What separates higher from lower performing firms in this localization process is their approach to learning. Higher performing firms are confident in the abilities of their local staff and are willing to delegate authority, reflecting a belief in systematic training and development. Moreover, they are more attentive to learning cues and moments, and correspondingly are able to monitor the localization process.

Go beyond the traditional belief of simply hiring locals. To succeed, firms now have to train and develop them

As indicated, a good part of any learning process is not simply adding to one's arsenal of knowledge, but also letting go of old thinking. In the past, it was efficient to bring in savvy and experienced expatriates to a new staging ground, because it was presumed that one's diversity in life's experiences could be leveraged well as strengths in any "catch-up" circumstances. For the most part, this was true.

However, more recent experiences began to contravene this old wisdom, because deep experiences took on the form of ethnocentric blinders that lulled people into thinking that local demands would simply fold into mainstream experiences. In this study, we noted that one prime difference between higher and lower performing firms was not only their approaches to delegation, but also their perceptions of the importance of local markets to their overall strategy. Perceptions of local autonomy vary considerably, with higher performing firms more willing to decentralize. Moreover, beliefs about the potential of emerging markets demarcate different levels of performance. Those who considered emerging markets as consequential to future performance are more likely to be in higher performing groups, as opposed to those who considered emerging markets to have less potential for growth.

Facets of localization are reflected in many strategic decisions. Modes of expansion differ by performance; higher performing firms are more likely to select partnerships/alliances; local sales teams; and mergers and acquisitions as modes of expansion. However, localization is not taken for granted. Higher performing firms see unsupportive local cultures and inadequate governance as primary internal barriers; lower performing firms view fixed costs, governance issues, and pressure from HQ as key internal barriers. In short, higher performing firms are more likely to invest in local talent and capabilities than are lower performing firms.

In order to manage profitable growth in the future, develop a systemic strategy for identifying growth segments and exploring opportunities for "scaling the tail"

Achieving profitable growth may be a complex process, but it can be managed effectively. The P-E-C Framework can be helpful as a roadmap for attaining this objective. In terms of positioning, the firm should assess how to capitalize on various sources of differentiation. In areas or regions where a middle class is thriving, or exhibits a potential for doing so, the firm can position itself by exploring product areas in which high-end or power brands can be meaningfully positioned. A portfolio of brands is desired because consumers have a tendency to switch among high-end brands. Because the consumer tends to be fledgling and insecure about choices, building brand loyalty might not be as developed with ("pull" strategy) advertising; instead, "push" strategies (distribution outlets) might be key.

In terms of the P-E-C, the second phase consists of defining and cultivating specific drivers to enhance any differentiation advantage. Traditionally, there are the marketing drivers, such as price points, branding, advertising, and distribution outlets. However, what differentiates higher and lower performing firms is their approach to localization. Specifically, higher performing firms take a proactive strategy toward training and delegating their local staff, and balancing against extreme localization by systemic learning.

Finally, per the P-E-C Framework, firms must develop supportive management systems to undergird their strategic decisions. A good part of successful implementation is appropriate training of local staff and judicious delegation. Another critical phase is developing a performance-based corporate culture. Without a good plan for strategic implementation, even well-conceived strategies will not be successful.

To the extent that all of these factors are realized, the requirements for "scaling the tail" can be fulfilled. While the former template emphasized the selection of mass consumption markets for commodity products, the changing game in consumer goods and retailing is more oriented at the development of a cluster of high-end brands for targeted middle-class segments, and then rigorously developing these segments through balanced localization. Such a scaling-in process will yield significant benefits that exemplify how building around peripheral niches can eventually lead to high growth and high profits.

In conclusion, global shifts provide graphic testimony that the future of emerging markets is a highly promising one. Even so, succeeding in these markets is no longer guaranteed by previously successful templates. Subtle changes in institutions, cultures, environments, and people have shifted advantage from traditional multinationals to astute local competitors that have used strong connections and deep knowledge of the local environment to build competitive advantage. Such changes have also laid the foundation for a new basis of growth based on different conceptions of scaling. Already, some of these local competitors have become global. To achieve profitable growth, multinationals have to match the intensity and passion of local competitors with new strategies that capitalize on their own resources and competencies.

In this book, we lay out a blueprint for how multinationals might be able to capitalize on opportunities, nurture their competencies, and leverage their traditional strengths. A prerequisite to success lies in the deep understanding of scale, the growth dynamics that underlie it, and nuances of emerging consumers in previously nascent market niches. While not discounting other reasons, our own advocacy based on the research on this book underscores the need to qualify any type of growth and not succumb to overgeneralization. Growth is important—even deserving of an overarching goal—but it should be tempered by considerations of scale, industry, resources, and context. Rather than an unqualified fetish, growth should provide a cautionary note in any consideration of corporate strategy.

Notes

1. Wikiinvest; see http://www.wikinvest.com/concept/Rise_of_China's_Middle_Class, p. 24.
2. Pankaj Ghemawat, "Developing global leaders," *McKinsey Quarterly* (June 2012).
3. Maria Letelier, Fernando Flores, and Charles Spinosa, "Developing productive consumers in emerging markets," *California Management Review*, 45(4), Product No. CMR263, 2003.

Appendices

Appendix I: participants in the field study

(There were 276 C-suite and senior executives who participated in the study. This appendix includes those who shared their insights and personal experience in a series of in-depth interviews with the project team. There are several individuals kept anonymous at their requests.)

TABLE A1.1 *Participants in the field study*

Company	Name	Position
Adidas Group	Edgar Ho	CFO, Greater China
Ajinomoto	Masayoshi Kurosaki	General Manager, Overseas Food and Seasoning Dept., Food Products Division
Asahi Group Holdings Ltd.	Naoki Izumiya	President and Representative Director
Beijing Hualian Hypermarket Co.	Anthony Y. Tasi	Chief Marketing and Innovation Office
Colgate Palmolive India	Godfrey Nthunzi	CFO
Danone	Pierre-Andre Terisse	CFO
Danone	Yves Pellegrino	Corporate Finance Director
Diageo	Anna Manz	Global Strategy Director
DT-Global Business Consulting	Dr. Daniel Thorniley	President
East.West.SBS Ltd.	David Steer	Managing Director
South Asia Institute, Harvard University	Tarun Khanna	Jorge Paulo Lemann Professor
IGD	Vicky Santani	Head of Asian Research
Kao	Motoki Ozaki	Chairman of the Board
Kirin Holdings	Senji Miyake	President and CEO
Mars	Ehab Abou Oaf	President, Asia Pacific
Molson Coors Cobra India	Rahul Goyal	CFO
GroupM	Swee Leng Ng	Group CFO and former CFO of Kraft Foods, China
Nestle	Jose Lopez	Executive Vice President
Sampoerna	Paul Janelle	President and Director
Procter & Gamble	Tapan Buch	CFO India
Al Futtaim Dubai Group	Jim McCallum	CEO of Robinsons and Head of Asia
Sapporo International	Yoshihiro Iwata	Director of Business Strategy Department
Suntory Beverage & Food Aisa	Henry Park	Chief Executive Officer
University of Cambridge	Navi Radjou	Fellow at Judge Business School

Appendix II: survey questionnaire

Introduction: understanding approaches to profitable growth in Asia

Growing successfully in Asia is critical to the long-term health of multinational consumer products firms and retailers. This 15-minute Economist Intelligence Unit survey on behalf of a global professional services firm is intended to assess the challenges that these companies face in building their businesses in Asian markets and the strategy they favor in overcoming these challenges.

The Economist Intelligence Unit is committed to protecting your privacy. Your personal details and company name will not be shared with any third party, including the survey sponsor.

Thank you for taking part.

Privacy Policy

Do you work in a country or regional leadership role in Asia for a multinational consumer products firm or a multinational retailer?
O   Yes, multinational consumer products
O   Yes, multinational retailer
O   No

What are your organization's global annual revenues in U.S. dollars?
O   Less than $100m
O   Between $100m and $500m
O   Between $500m and $1bn
O   Between $1bn and $10bn
O   Between $10bn and $25bn
O   More than $25bn

In which country are you personally based?
O   China
O   India
O   Indonesia
O   Japan
O   Malaysia
O   Philippines
O   Singapore
O   South Korea

○ Taiwan
○ Thailand
○ Vietnam
○ Other, please specify_____

Section I

Note: Unless stated otherwise, please answer all questions from the perspective of the local operating unit, not the global corporate.

1 Which of the following metrics or key performance indicators (KPIs) have been the most important measure of your company's performance in the local market? And which do you expect to be most important over the next three years? Please rank the options from 1 to 3 for each column (where 1 is most important).

TABLE AII.1 *Survey question 1*

	Currently	Next three years
Revenue growth	☐	☐
Market share growth	☐	☐
Operating profit	☐	☐

2 Over the past few years, to what extent have changes in the following factors impacted your business? Please rate 1 to 5, where 1 is a significant decrease in impact and 5 is a significant increase in impact.

TABLE AII.2 *Survey question 2*

	Significant decrease in impact		No change		Significant increase in impact
	1	2	3	4	5
Volatility of market demand	☐	☐	☐	☐	☐
Competition from local firms	☐	☐	☐	☐	☐
Competition from multinational firms	☐	☐	☐	☐	☐
Local market regulation	☐	☐	☐	☐	☐
Pressure from global HQ to deliver growth and profit	☐	☐	☐	☐	☐
Changes in local consumer/shopper behaviors and preferences	☐	☐	☐	☐	☐

3 How do you believe your company is performing in the local market/region for which you are responsible compared with your closest competitors across the following metrics? Please rate 1 to 5, where 1 is significantly worse, 2 is slightly worse, 3 is similar, 4 is slightly better, and 5 is significantly better.

TABLE AII.3 *Survey question 3*

	Significantly worse 1	Slightly worse 2	Similar 3	Slightly better 4	Significantly better 5	Don't know
Market share position	☐	☐	☐	☐	☐	☐
Profitability	☐	☐	☐	☐	☐	☐
Revenue growth	☐	☐	☐	☐	☐	☐

4 How does the current performance of your company in the local market/region for which you are responsible compare with your company's performance globally? Please rate 1 to 5, where 1 is significantly worse and 5 is significantly better.

TABLE AII.4 *Survey question 4*

	Significantly worse 1	2	3	4	Significantly better 5	Don't know
Revenue growth rates	☐	☐	☐	☐	☐	☐
Profitability	☐	☐	☐	☐	☐	☐

5 Which sources of finance are currently the most important for your local market investments and which do you expect to be most important in the next three years? Select up to two options for each column.

TABLE AII.5 *Survey question 5*

	Currently	Next three years
Profits from local operations	☐	☐
External capital raised locally	☐	☐
Capital from headquarters	☐	☐
Other, please specify_____	☐	☐

6 Which of the following best describes your treatment of profits that you make in the local market? Please select one only.
   ○ We invest all of our profits in building the local market business
   ○ We invest some of our profits in building the local market business, and return some to corporate headquarters
   ○ We return all our profits to corporate headquarters
   ○ We are neither investing profits in the local business nor returning profit to corporate headquarters
   ○ We have not reached profitability

7 To what extent do you agree or disagree with the following statements? Select one column in each row.

TABLE AII.6 *Survey question 7*

	Strongly agree	Somewhat agree	Neither agree nor disagree	Somewhat disagree	Strongly disagree
Emerging markets will become the main engine of growth for our company globally in the next three years	☐	☐	☐	☐	☐
Emerging markets will become the main engine of profit for our company globally in the next three years	☐	☐	☐	☐	☐
Our global company can only succeed if we focus our emerging market investments in a few priority markets	☐	☐	☐	☐	☐
To succeed in emerging markets, we need to adapt our products to meet the needs of local consumers	☐	☐	☐	☐	☐
To succeed in emerging markets, we need to adapt our global operating model to meet the needs of local consumers	☐	☐	☐	☐	☐
Different regions within the local market require different strategies	☐	☐	☐	☐	☐

TABLE AII.6 Continued

	Strongly agree	Somewhat agree	Neither agree nor disagree	Somewhat disagree	Strongly disagree
To maximise synergies, we need to identify similar markets and manage our local operations in those markets as a cluster/group	☐	☐	☐	☐	☐

Section II: Consumer products

8   Which of the following best describes your company's primary strategy in the local market in which you currently operate? Please select one for each row.

TABLE AII.7 Survey question 8

Focusing on one or two core product categories	☐	☐	Participating in multiple product categories
Targeting established product categories	☐	☐	Creating new product categories
Mainly selling low-cost products	☐	☐	Mainly selling premium priced products
Mainly selling products developed for the local market	☐	☐	Mainly selling global products
Creating local brand(s)	☐	☐	Using/adapting global brand(s)
Manufacturing products locally	☐	☐	Importing products
Leveraging local R&D/product development	☐	☐	Leveraging global R&D/product development
Focusing on priority territories within local markets	☐	☐	Selling nationally
Building own distribution network	☐	☐	Using third-party distribution network

9   Which of the following modes of expansion have been most important in growing your local business? Select up to three that apply.
   - Establishing local sales team
   - Establishing local manufacturing
   - Entering into partnerships/alliances
   - M&A—majority control
   - Minority equity investment
   - Franchise/licensing
   - Other, please specify_____

134   *Appendices*

10 Which sales channels do you use in the market that you manage? Select one option for each row.

TABLE AII.8   *Survey question 10*

	Don't use	Marginally use	Significantly use
Traditional trade (e.g., mom and pops, market stalls)	☐	☐	☐
Modern trade (e.g., chain supermarkets)	☐	☐	☐
Own/exclusive retail outlets	☐	☐	☐
Direct to consumer: door to door	☐	☐	☐
Direct to consumer: digital (own)	☐	☐	☐
Digital (third-party e-commerce)	☐	☐	☐
Vending machines	☐	☐	☐

11 Which of the following do you consider to have been your main sources of competitive advantage in your local market? Select up to three.
   ○ Price point
   ○ Product quality
   ○ Product range
   ○ Product innovation
   ○ Brand strength
   ○ Distribution footprint
   ○ Sales service
   ○ Marketing
   ○ Workforce
   ○ Local consumer understanding
   ○ Local relationships (government, retailers, suppliers, etc.)
   ○ Cost control
   ○ Supply chain
   ○ Other, please specify_____

12 Which of the following approaches will be most important in growing your revenues locally over the next three years? Select up to three.
   ○ Launching new products/services in current categories
   ○ Launching new products/services in new categories
   ○ Innovating existing products
   ○ Raising prices
   ○ Lowering prices

- Increasing marketing spending
- Realigning marketing spending
- Utilizing new distribution channels
- Expanding reach of distribution
- Improving sales service support
- Other, please specify_____

13 Which of the following cost reduction measures does your company consider the most important tools for improving margins? Select up to three.
- Centralization and the creation of shared service centers
- Use of lean manufacturing/Six Sigma and other techniques
- Outsourcing of non-core competencies
- Headcount reduction (job cuts)
- Strategic sourcing and centralization of procurement
- Localizing manufacturing
- Optimization of supply chain network (manufacturing and distribution)
- Standardization of manufacturing technologies/processes
- Other, please specify_____

14 What input does local management have on business decisions impacting your local market? For each row, please rate the decision-making input of local management on a range spanning 'complete autonomy' to 'no influence over decisions'.

TABLE AII.9 *Survey question 14*

	Complete autonomy	Some influence over decisions	No influence over decisions
Product development	☐	☐	☐
Product range	☐	☐	☐
Headcount changes	☐	☐	☐
Branding decisions	☐	☐	☐
Setting targets and KPIs	☐	☐	☐
Supply chain investments	☐	☐	☐
Forming local partnerships and alliances	☐	☐	☐
M&A	☐	☐	☐
Choosing suppliers	☐	☐	☐
Choice of channels/route to market decisions	☐	☐	☐

15 Where does each of the following functions reside in relation to your local operation? Select all that apply.

TABLE AII.10 *Survey question 15*

	Local/ In country	Regional/Cluster	Global
R&D	☐	☐	☐
Sales	☐	☐	☐
Marketing	☐	☐	☐
Manufacturing	☐	☐	☐
Procurement	☐	☐	☐
Supply chain planning	☐	☐	☐
Distribution	☐	☐	☐
Finance	☐	☐	☐
IT	☐	☐	☐
HR	☐	☐	☐
Strategy	☐	☐	☐

16 Which of the following external factors do you see as the biggest barriers to your company's profitable growth? Select up to three.
- Labor and input cost inflation
- Price erosion and demand decline
- Market fragmentation
- Exchange rate fluctuation
- Inadequate marketing channels
- Competitive pressure
- Poor physical infrastructure
- Insufficient data (market, point of sale)
- Cost and availability of distribution channels
- Increased regulatory and compliance requirements
- Restrictions on market access
- Tax burden
- Other, please specify_____

17 Which of the following internal factors do you see as the biggest barriers to your company's profitable growth? Select up to three.
- Inadequate supply chain infrastructure
- Lack of pricing power
- Weak IT system
- Lack of talent/capabilities
- Inadequate governance
- Too many fixed costs

○ Interest on and/or servicing debt
○ Access to capital
○ Unsupportive local corporate culture
○ Pressure from corporate headquarters
○ Other, please specify_____

Section III: retail

18 Which of the following best describes your company's primary strategy in the local market in which you currently operate?

TABLE AII.11 *Survey question 18*
Please select one for each row.

Focusing on one or two core product categories	☐	☐	Participating in multiple product categories
Developing existing product categories	☐	☐	Creating new product categories
Mainly selling value priced products	☐	☐	Mainly selling premium priced products
Mainly selling locally sourced products	☐	☐	Mainly selling globally sourced products
Creating local brand propositions	☐	☐	Using global brand propositions consistently
Selling few own-label products	☐	☐	Selling significant own-label products
Focusing on priority territories within local market	☐	☐	Selling nationally

19 Which of the following modes of expansion have been most important in growing your local business? Select up to three.
   ○ Partnership/alliance
   ○ M&A—majority control
   ○ Minority equity investment
   ○ Franchise/licensing
   ○ Greenfield investments
   ○ Other, please specify_____

20 Which retail formats do you operate? Select all that apply.
   ○ Convenience stores
   ○ Neighborhood stores (e.g., supermarkets)
   ○ Hypermarkets

- Boutiques (e.g., mall stores)
- Department stores
- Cash and carries/wholesalers
- Discount stores
- Online/digital (e-commerce)
- Specialty store
- Other, please specify_____

21 What do you consider to have been your main sources of competitive advantage in your local market? Select up to three.
- Price point
- Product or service quality
- Product width/depth
- Brand strength
- Marketing
- Local shopper understanding
- Workforce
- Cost control
- Economies of scale
- Supply chain
- Local relationships (government, suppliers, etc.)
- Other, please specify_____

22 Which of the following approaches will be most important in growing your revenues locally over the next three years? Select up to three.
- Opening new stores in current geographies
- Opening new stores in new geographies (expanding geographic reach)
- Selling new product categories/services
- Launching new brick and mortar formats (e.g., supermarket chain opening convenience stores)
- Selling products online
- Lowering prices
- Introducing/offering a loyalty scheme
- Increasing marketing spend
- Realigning marketing spend
- Other, please specify_____

23 Which of the following cost reduction measures does your company consider the most important tools for improving margins? Select up to three.
   ○ Centralization and the creation of shared service centers
   ○ Use of lean/Six Sigma and other techniques
   ○ Outsourcing of non-core competencies
   ○ Headcount reduction and efficiency drives
   ○ Strategic sourcing and centralization of procurement
   ○ Changes to the operating model and organizational structure to reduce overhead costs and standardize business service and delivery
   ○ Optimization of marketing and advertising spend
   ○ Optimization of supply chain network
   ○ Other, please specify_____

24 What input does local management have in business decisions impacting your local market? For each row, please rate the decision-making input of local management on a range spanning 'complete autonomy' to 'no influence over decisions'.

TABLE AII.12 Survey question 24

	Complete autonomy	Some influence over decisions	No influence over decisions
Product range/service offering	☐	☐	☐
Format choices	☐	☐	☐
Own-label strategies	☐	☐	☐
Headcount changes	☐	☐	☐
Branding decisions	☐	☐	☐
Setting targets and KPIs	☐	☐	☐
Technology investments	☐	☐	☐
Supply chain investments	☐	☐	☐
Forming local partnerships and alliances	☐	☐	☐
Choosing suppliers	☐	☐	☐

25 Where does each of the following functions reside in relation to your local operation? Select all that apply.

TABLE AII.13 Survey question 25

	Local/ In country	Regional/ Cluster	Global
Marketing	☐	☐	☐
Buying	☐	☐	☐
Store development	☐	☐	☐

Continued

TABLE AII.13 *Continued*

	Local/ In country	Regional/ Cluster	Global
Finance	☐	☐	☐
IT	☐	☐	☐
HR	☐	☐	☐
Strategy	☐	☐	☐

26 Which of the following external factors do you see as the biggest barriers to your company's profitable growth?
Select up to three.
○ Labor and commodity inflation
○ Demand decline
○ Market fragmentation
○ Exchange rate fluctuation
○ Competitive pressure
○ Poor physical infrastructure
○ Insufficient data (market, point of sale)
○ Logistics cost
○ Increased regulatory and compliance requirements
○ Restrictions on market access
○ Tax burden
○ Other, please specify_____

27 Which of the following internal factors do you see as the biggest barriers to your company's profitable growth?
Select up to three.
○ Inadequate supply chain infrastructure
○ Lack of bargaining power
○ Incomplete/inconsistent data/IT
○ Lack of talent/capabilities
○ Inadequate governance
○ Too many fixed costs
○ Interest on and/or servicing debt
○ Access to capital
○ Unsupportive local corporate culture
○ Pressure from corporate headquarters
○ Other, please specify_____

Section IV

28 To what extent do you agree or disagree with the following statements? Select one column in each row.

TABLE AII.14 *Survey question 28*

	Strongly agree	Somewhat agree	Neither agree nor disagree	Somewhat disagree	Strongly disagree
We endeavor to predict most market changes and control their impact with good decisions	☐	☐	☐	☐	☐
We have a formal planning approach which is aligned to strategy throughout the entire organization	☐	☐	☐	☐	☐
We control our circumstances by developing managers who are comfortable with change and building flexibility and resilience to cope with unpredictability and changes in demand	☐	☐	☐	☐	☐
The unpredictability of the external environment means that we focus primarily on being cost-competitive so that we can quickly recover from an unexpected change	☐	☐	☐	☐	☐

29 Which approach will you most emphasise in building your local management team over the next three years? Please rate 1 to 5, where 1 is least important and 5 is most important.

TABLE AII.15 *Survey question 29*

	Least important 1	2	3	4	Most important 5
Build from within the local company	☐	☐	☐	☐	☐
Hire local talent from other organizations	☐	☐	☐	☐	☐
Use expatriates from parent company	☐	☐	☐	☐	☐
Hire expatriates from other organizations	☐	☐	☐	☐	☐

30 How effective do you consider your local management team to be at managing the following aspects of its business? Please rate 1 to 5, where 1 is not at all effective and 5 is very effective.

TABLE AII.16 *Survey question 30*

	Not at all effective				Very effective
	1	2	3	4	5
Addressing local consumer needs	☐	☐	☐	☐	☐
Tailoring operating model to needs of local markets	☐	☐	☐	☐	☐
Competing with low-cost local competitors	☐	☐	☐	☐	☐
Anticipating and responding to market volatility	☐	☐	☐	☐	☐
Developing local talent	☐	☐	☐	☐	☐
Understanding the local political and regulatory environment	☐	☐	☐	☐	☐
Empowering employees to make decisions	☐	☐	☐	☐	☐
Cultivating a performance-oriented corporate culture	☐	☐	☐	☐	☐
Ensuring visibility of financial and operational information	☐	☐	☐	☐	☐
Coordinating with broader global operations	☐	☐	☐	☐	☐

About you

Which job title most closely matches your role?
- Country manager
- President
- Company secretary
- Senior partner
- Vice president
- Senior director
- Head of finance
- Head of marketing
- Other, please specify _____

How long has your company been operating in your local market?
- Less than 2 years
- Between 2 and 5 years
- Between 5 and 10 years
- Between 10 and 50 years
- More than 50 years

What are your organization's annual revenues in U.S. dollars for your local market?
○ Less than $50m
○ Between $50m and $200m
○ Between $200m and $500m
○ Between $500m and $1bn
○ More than $1bn

What is your company's main subsector?
○ Food
○ Beverage
○ Home and Personal Care
○ Tobacco
○ Apparel
○ Grocery retail
○ Other retail
○ Other consumer goods

Appendix III: demographics of survey participants

A survey questionnaire was designed, and it was continuously revised to accommodate the scope of the study. In the process of finalizing the survey, both research teams from IEMS and EY interviewed a number of field managers from Asia, incorporating their ideas and feedback. The final questionnaire was sent to a targeted sample that had been pre-analyzed for performance. The Economist Unit administered the survey; anonymity of respondents was guaranteed. A total of 253 respondents from 10 countries completed the survey; demographics are presented in this appendix.

Survey demographics

The IEMS research team disaggregated the sample into four quadrants of varying performance levels: (1) high profits, high growth; (2) high profits, low growth; (3) low profits, high growth; and (4) low profits, low growth. The intent was to examine fine-grained differences between these quadrants. In addition, the sample was subjected to different combinations of varying profit and growth. As a variant of sensitivity analysis, we searched for significant differences in means and modalities across different combinations, and finally selected enduring findings across all these levels.

To be clear, low performance does *not* mean poor performance, but rather performance that is low relative to others. Thus, in the ensuing analysis, the attributions are labeled "higher performing" and "lower performing," respectively. In our final analysis, we compared higher performing (n=133) versus lower performing (n = 63) firms.

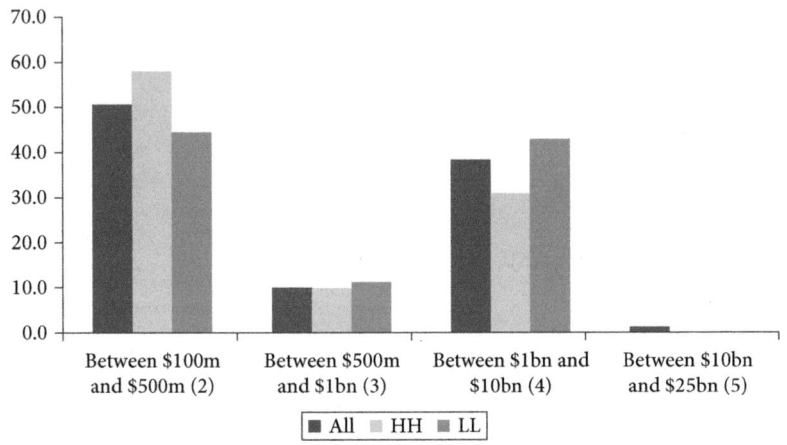

FIGURE AIII.1   *Parent firm global sales*

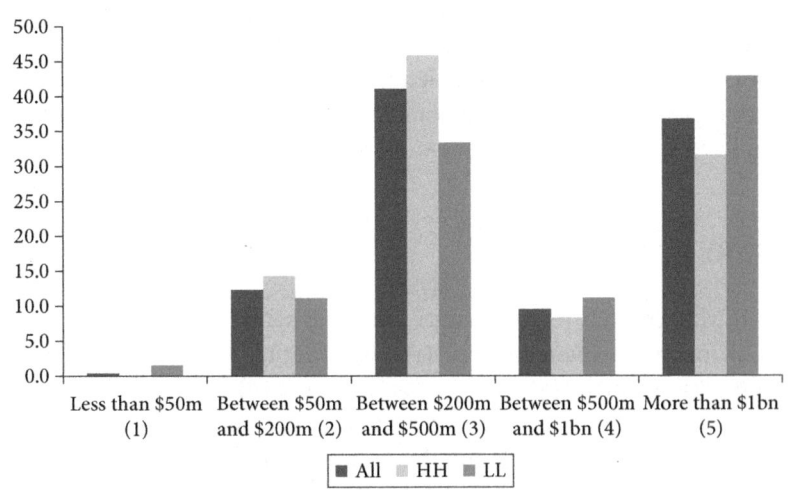

FIGURE AIII.2   *Subsidiary local sales*

Appendices 145

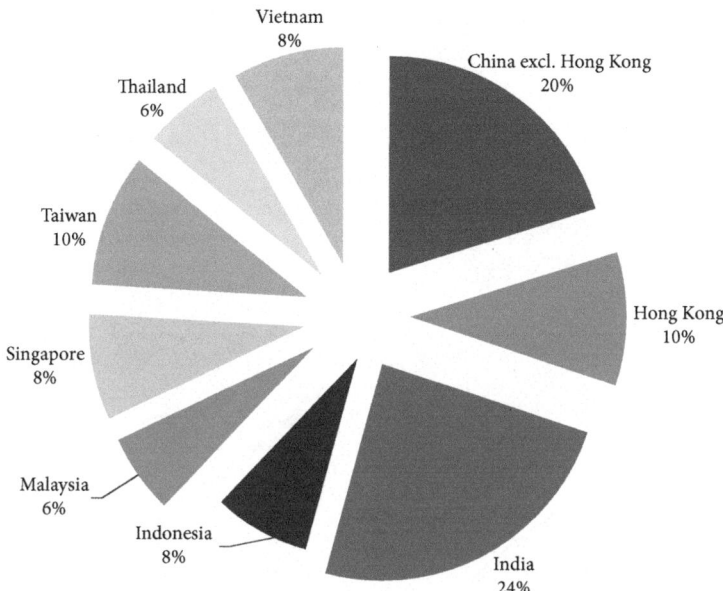

FIGURE AIII.3 *Country representation of survey sample*

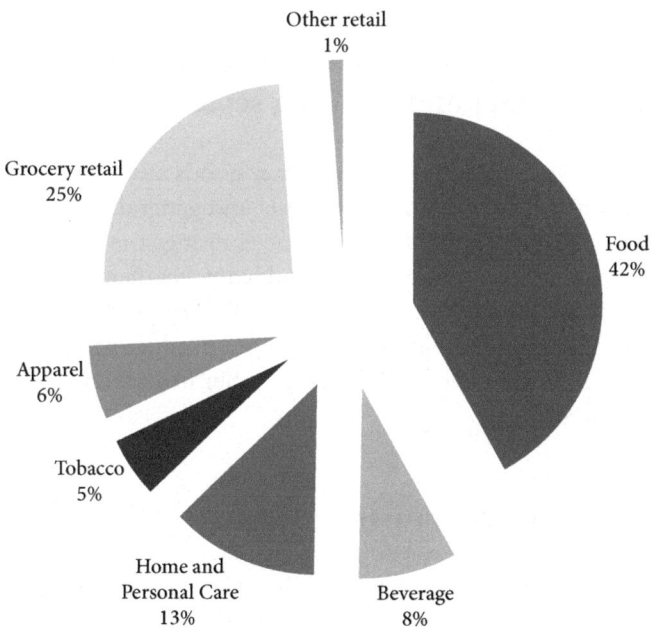

FIGURE AIII.4 *Industry representation of survey sample*

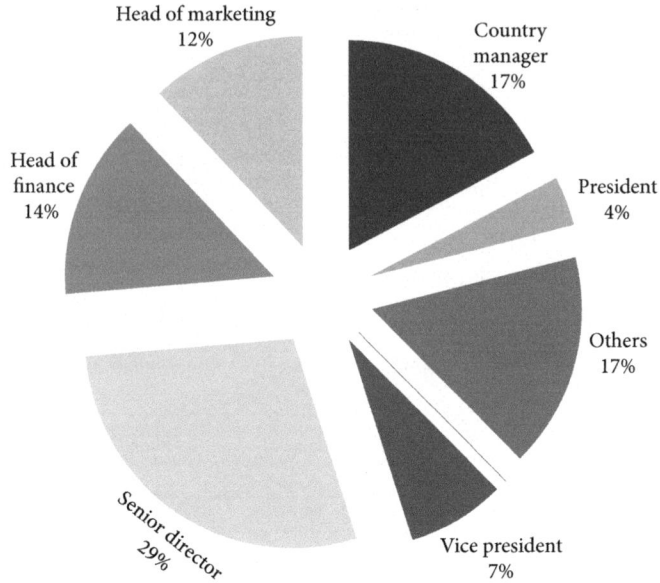

FIGURE AIII.5   *Respondents by job titles*

Appendix IV: performance analysis of MNCs in Asia in consumer and retailing sectors[1]

In this study, we focused on the consumer goods and retailing sectors of emerging markets for which our analysis and generalizations are based. While we acknowledge that this can be limiting, the consumer goods and retailing sectors comprise a significant segment of production. Moreover, it is a segment in which we can discern pockets of opportunities and evaluate the potential of individual product categories and the performance of profitable growth versus other firms. Here is a summary of the appraisal.

Part 1: descriptive statistics

In order to understand the performance of foreign firms in the consumer product and retail industries in Asia, we selected data from ORBIS for all firms in the following industries:

10—Manufacture of food products,
11—Manufacture of beverages,
12—Manufacture of tobacco products,
1520—Manufacture of footwear,
204—Manufacture of soap and detergents, cleaning and polishing preparations, perfumes and toilet preparations,
463—Wholesale of food, beverages, and tobacco,
472—Retail sale of food, beverages and tobacco in specialized stores,
4775—Retail sale of cosmetic and toilet articles in specialized stores,
4781—Retail sale via stalls and markets of food, beverages, and tobacco products.

We then calculated the five-year average (from 2006 to 2010) sales growth and ROA for each industry in each country.

Cross-sectional data by country and sectors

TABLE AIV.1 *Sales growth for the overall sample**

	China	India	Malaysia	Indonesia	Thailand	Singapore	Vietnam	Average	N
Food	39.53	17.39	12.04	22.49	16.20	23.57	23.34	22.08	54,576
Beverage	36.73	25.34	24.31	13.42	17.55	8.91	5.22	18.78	7,362
Tobacco	24.09	21.49	1.61	16.81	11.24	11.95	19.85	15.29	358
Footwear	27.98	5.04	28.93	17.86	9.45	50.07	49.02	26.91	9,634
Healthcare	27.11	11.56	7.57	18.87	16.54	28.07	23.12	18.98	2,948
Retail	40.07	23.52	12.51	16.45	14.44	23.17	27.39	22.51	19,865
Average	32.59	17.39	14.50	17.65	14.24	24.29	24.66	20.76	
N	83,240	1,751	1,836	2,667	4,100	214	935		94,743

Note: *In percentage

The footwear industry enjoys the highest growth rate during the study period (2006–2010), with average sales growth of 26.91% across these seven countries, followed by the food and retail industries with a small gap (around 4%). The next group consists of the beverage and healthcare industries, with average sales growth around 19%. Tobacco is the laggard, with only 15.29% average growth rate, perhaps due to the fact that people in these countries tend to be increasingly concerned about health problems caused by smoking.

China is leading the growth, with an annual sales growth rate of 32.59%, well ahead of other countries. Vietnam and Singapore belong to the second group, with 7% lower than China. Indonesia and India form the third group, with an average growth rate around 17.50%. Malaysia and Thailand constitute the last group, with average sales growth around 14%.

The overall sales growth of the sample firms across these industries and countries is 20.76%, implying that a firm doubles its size every 3.52 years.

TABLE AIV.2 *Profitability for the overall sample**

	China	India	Malaysia	Indonesia	Thailand	Singapore	Vietnam	Average	N
Food	14.15	0.93	6.66	4.41	0.54	6.79	8.01	5.93	54,576
Beverage	11.75	−0.87	5.11	4.53	2.28	7.03	3.67	4.79	7,362
Tobacco	8.53	6.23	10.98	9.29	1.23	2.00	5.20	6.21	358
Footwear	10.33	−0.46	8.00	−0.52	1.27	25.60	8.84	7.58	9,634
Healthcare	7.93	6.60	8.84	15.15	−0.28	13.43	20.85	10.36	2,948
Retail	4.91	−1.36	5.29	0.20	0.03	9.61	6.65	3.62	19,865
Average	9.60	1.85	7.48	5.51	0.85	10.74	8.87	6.41	
N	83,240	1,751	1,836	2,667	4,100	214	935		94,743

Note: *In percentage

In terms of profit, the healthcare industry ranks the first, with annual average ROA of 10.36% across the countries, followed by footwear, tobacco, food, beverage, and retail. Retail is the laggard, with average ROA of only 3.62%.

Singapore leads in profitability, with an annual average ROA of 10.74%, followed by China with average ROA of 9.60%. Malaysia and Vietnam form the second group, with average ROA around 7%–8%. India and Thailand are the laggards, with average ROA of only around 1%. The average ROA of firms in these industries is 6.41%.

In sum, footwear is the most desirable industry, with the highest sales growth and relatively high profit. The healthcare industry is also desirable because of its high profitability. China is the most attractive place to operate, with the highest sales growth and the second highest profit. Singapore and Vietnam are the second best choices, with relatively high sales growth and profit. India and Indonesia enjoy a high sales growth rate, but low profit whereas Malaysia is the opposite, with low sales growth, but relatively high profit. Thailand is the laggard, with the lowest sales growth and profit among the seven countries.

Descriptive statistics for foreign firms

Next, we examined the performance of foreign firms in these countries and in these industries.

TABLE AIV.3 *Sales growth for foreign firms**

	China	India	Malaysia	Indonesia	Thailand	Singapore	Vietnam	Average	N
Food	27.65	9.91	17.31	19.49	15.00	25.13	n.a.	19.08	1,582
Beverage	23.78	27.25	13.23	12.64	20.57	n.a.	n.a.	19.49	226
Tobacco	17.52	34.92	9.57	2.68	n.a.	2.70	n.a.	13.48	20
Footwear	15.92	n.a.	50.28	−3.76	n.a.	n.a.	n.a.	20.81	770
Healthcare	12.95	15.53	9.59	11.94	14.27	24.42	n.a.	14.78	180
Retail	69.92	12.32	11.79	−1.15	9.44	29.13	n.a.	21.91	268
Average	27.96	19.99	18.63	6.97	14.82	20.35	n.a.	18.26	
N	2,540	92	146	78	120	70			3,046

Note: *In percentage

Comparing Table AIV.1 and Table AIV.3, there emerges a pattern of sales growth for foreign firms. In general, the average sales growth for foreign firms is slightly lower: 18.26% for foreign firms versus 20.76% for all firms. This holds true for five out of the six industries, except beverage. The average sales growth rate of foreign firms in the beverage industry is 19.49%, compared with 18.78% for all firms.

In terms of country, foreign firms in China, Indonesia, and Singapore grow more slowly than other firms. For India, Malaysia, and Thailand, foreign firms outgrow other firms. The most striking difference between foreign and other firms in terms of sales growth is the retail industry in China: while foreign retailers enjoy average sales growth of around 70%, the same number for other firms is only 40%. The place where foreign firms underperform other firms the most is the footwear industry in Indonesia: while foreign firms have an average sales growth of around 3.76%, the number for other firms is around 18%.

TABLE AIV.4 *Profitability for foreign firms**

	China	India	Malaysia	Indonesia	Thailand	Singapore	Vietnam	Average	N
Food	8.20	1.24	9.67	5.85	8.64	8.85	n.a.	7.08	1,582
Beverage	4.12	1.20	14.86	18.28	12.52	1.00	n.a.	8.66	226
Tobacco	11.60	4.62	18.78	0.87	n.a.	0.14	n.a.	7.20	20
Footwear	5.50	n.a.	17.33	−4.67	n.a.	n.a.	n.a.	6.05	770
Healthcare	7.32	17.30	13.35	19.11	12.33	11.10	n.a.	13.42	180
Retail	2.84	n.a.	9.92	−7.00	3.12	10.42	n.a.	3.86	268
Average	6.60	6.09	13.99	5.41	9.15	6.30	n.a.	7.92	
N	2,540	92	146	78	120	70			3,046

Note: *In percentage

Next, we compare Table AIV.2 and Table AIV.4 for foreign firm profits. Foreign firms enjoy higher ROA than other firms (7.92% vs. 6.41%). This pattern holds true for all industries, except for footwear, where foreign firms have lower profit than other firms (6.05% vs. 7.58%). In terms of national differences, China and Singapore are the exceptions, where foreign firms have lower profit than other firms. In Indonesia, the profits for foreign and other firms are similar. In India, Malaysia, and Thailand, foreign firms have much higher profit than other firms. In Thailand, in particular, foreign firms have an average ROA of 9.15%, compared to 0.85% of all firms. The place where foreign firms outperform other firms the most in terms of ROA is the beverage industry in Indonesia: while other firms have an average ROA of around 4.53%, the number for foreign firms is 18.28%.

To summarize, foreign firms in general have slower sales growth, but higher profit, than other firms. Although Chinese and Singaporean firms enjoy high sales growth and high profit, foreign firms in these countries have much lower performance in sales growth and profit. On the contrary, foreign firms in India, Malaysia, and Thailand enjoy higher sales growth and profit than other firms.

Profitable Growth (PG) firms

Among foreign firms in these countries, we selected a group of foreign firms that achieved profitable growth during the study period (PG firms). The selection criteria are:

1. Select firms that have above five-year average sales growth and ROA by industry and by country.
2. Exclude domestic firms.
3. Exclude firms that are too small or have too many yearly missing values.

We arrived at a total of 35 firms in these countries (see the list in Table AIV.7). On average, they enjoy annual sales growth of 37.04% and annual ROA of 18.39%. The sales growth and profit of PG firms is higher than all firms, including both foreign and local firms. Given that foreign firms, in general, have slower sales growth, the high sales growth of PG firms is remarkable. In particular, in China, where foreign firms generally have slower sales growth and lower profit than other firms, PG firms enjoy annual sales growth of 82.58% and annual ROA of 17.20%, far ahead of other firms. The situation is similar for PG firms in other countries, although the difference is not as sharp as in China. For example, while foreign firms in India have only an average ROA of 6.09%, the number is 15.14% for PG firms in India. Overall, it is prudent to conclude that PG firms outperform both foreign firms and local firms in their respective countries and industries.

TABLE AIV.5 Sales growth for profitable growth firms*

	China	India	Malaysia	Indonesia	Thailand	Singapore	Vietnam	Average	N
Food	105.08	26.22	15.27	37.67	35.01	39.48	n.a.	43.12	12
Beverage	120.53	26.49	n.a.	20.06	18.88	n.a.	n.a.	46.49	5
Tobacco	n.a.	n.a.	12.41	n.a.	n.a.	n.a.	n.a.	12.41	1
Footwear	73.45	n.a.	n.a.	n.a.	n.a.	n.a.	n.a.	73.45	1
Healthcare	31.24	13.83	17.42	18.62	39.42	n.a.	n.a.	24.11	9
Retail	n.a.	n.a.	17.04	n.a.	21.79	29.21	n.a.	22.68	7
Average	82.58	22.18	15.54	25.45	28.78	34.35	n.a.	37.04	
N	7	6	6	4	9	3			35

Note: *In percentage

TABLE AIV.6 Profitability for profitable growth firms*

	China	India	Malaysia	Indonesia	Thailand	Singapore	Vietnam	Average	N
Food	26.85	17.14	27.20	8.83	19.60	11.40	n.a.	18.50	12
Beverage	18.71	0.50	n.a.	24.60	15.20	n.a.	n.a.	14.75	5
Tobacco	n.a.	n.a.	20.20	n.a.	n.a.	n.a.	n.a.	20.20	1
Footwear	13.75	n.a.	n.a.	n.a.	n.a.	n.a.	n.a.	13.75	1
Healthcare	9.50	27.79	29.50	38.20	12.87	n.a.	n.a.	23.57	9
Retail	n.a.	n.a.	22.63	n.a.	13.60	22.50	n.a.	19.58	7
Average	17.20	15.14	24.88	23.88	15.32	16.95	n.a.	18.39	
N	7	6	6	4	9	3	0		35

Note: *In percentage

TABLE AIV.7 List of profitable growth companies

Company	Location	Primary business	Average sales growth (%)	Average ROA (%)
Herbalife Healthcare Products	China	Food	161.04	18.60
Kangshifu (Shenyang) Beverage	China	Beverage	175.95	15.00
Ke Daily Necessities	China	Health Care	31.24	9.50
Lianjiang Qinglu Shoes	China	Foot ware	73.45	13.75
Givaudan Edible Essence Perfume	China	Food	88.67	22.33
Shanggaorui Wheat Food	China	Food	57.32	37.80

Continued

TABLE AIV.7 Continued

Company	Location	Primary business	Average sales growth (%)	Average ROA (%)
Tianjin Nestle Natural Mineral Water	China	Beverage	78.97	23.67
PT Cahaya Kalbar Tbk.	Indonesia	Food	40.24	5.20
PT Multi Bintang	Indonesia	Beverage	20.06	24.60
PT Unilever Indonesia Tbk.	Indonesia	Health Care	18.62	38.20
Sari Husada Tbk.	Indonesia	Food	23.02	27.00
Cadbury India, Ltd.	India	Food	18.21	13.75
Colgate Palmolive (India), Ltd.	India	Health Care	16.08	35.20
Hindustan Unilever, Ltd.	India	Health Care	11.79	24.20
Indo Nissin Foods, Ltd.	India	Food	35.90	6.80
Nestle India, Ltd.	India	Food	22.55	30.20
P&G Hygiene and Health Care, Ltd.	India	Health Care	13.49	23.00
Campbell Soup Southeast Asia	Malaysia	Retail	22.80	29.67
Clorox (Malaysia) Sdn Bhd.	Malaysia	Health Care	17.42	29.50
F&N Beverages Marketing Bhd.	Malaysia	Retail	14.74	18.40
JT International Berhad	Malaysia	Tobacco	12.41	20.20
Kraft Malaysia Sdn. Bhd.	Malaysia	Food	21.37	31.50
Unilever (Malaysia) Holding	Malaysia	Food	12.22	24.33
Japan Foods Holding, Ltd.	Singapore	Retail	32.10	16.80
Kencana Agri, Ltd.	Singapore	Food	39.48	11.40
LVMH Fragrances and Cosmetics	Singapore	Retail	26.32	28.20
Ab Food & Beverages, Ltd.	Thailand	Beverage	18.51	24.00
Amway (Thailand), Ltd.	Thailand	Retail	18.18	18.40
Kerry Ingredients (Thailand) Co.	Thailand	Food	35.01	19.60
L'Oreal (Thailand), Ltd.	Thailand	Health Care	21.02	13.00
Lion Corporation (Thailand), Ltd.	Thailand	Health Care	19.71	8.60
Mckey Food Services, Ltd.	Thailand	Retail	21.25	14.40
Perrier Vittel (Thailand), Ltd.	Thailand	Beverage	19.24	6.40
Wyeth (Thailand), Ltd.	Thailand	Retail	25.93	8.00
Yamahatsu (Thailand), Ltd.	Thailand	Health Care	77.53	17.00

Note

1 We are grateful to Dr. Nan Zhou for her input in preparing this technical note.

Bibliography

Ács, Z. J. & Attila V. "Entrepreneurship, agglomeration and technological change." *Small Business Economics*, 1992. 24(2):115–138.

Anderson, C. *The Long Tail: Why the Future of Business Is Selling Less for More* (New York: Hyperion Books, 2006).

Atsmon, Y., Kloss, M., & Smit, S. "Parsing the growth advantage of emerging-market companies." *McKinsey Quarterly* (May 2012). http://www.mckinsey.com/insights/strategy/parsing_the_growth_advantage_of_emerging-market_companies.

Avery, J. & Norton, M. "Learning from extreme customers." *Harvard Business Review*, (January 6, 2014).

Baghai, M., Smit, S., & Patrick S. V. McKinsey Solutions Report, "Granular growth: granular growth is a unique approach to assessing growth performance and developing robust growth strategies." http://solutions.mckinsey.com/granulargrowth.

Best, R. J. *Market-Based Management: Strategies for Growing Consumer Value and Profitability* (Upper Saddle River, NJ: Prentice Hall, 1999).

Borg, I. & Groenen. P. *Modern Multidimensional Scaling: Theory and Applications* (2d ed.) (New York: Springer-Verlag, 2005), pp. 207–212.

Buckley, C. "How a Revolution becomes a Dinner Party: Stratification, Mobility, and the New Rich in Urban China." In *Culture and Privilege in Capitalist Asia*. Michael Pinches, ed. (New York: Routledge, 1999).

Buzzell, R.D. & Gale, B.T. *The PIMS Principles: Linking Strategy to Performance* (New York: Free Press, 1987).

Chattopadhyay, A. & Batra, R. *The Emerging Market Multinationals* (New York: McGraw Hill, 2012).

"Coming of age," *Economist* (January 19, 2006). http://www.economist.com/node/5411977.

Deloitte & Touche. "In pursuit of profitable growth: restructuring an operating model for emerging markets." Deloitte & Touche Report. 2011. https://www.deloitte.com/assets/Dcom-UnitedStates/Local%20Assets/Documents/us_consulting_emergingmarketsrestructuring_062111.pdf.

EY (with Wilson, W.T.), "Middle class growth in emerging markets: Hitting the sweet spot," 2012; http://www.ey.com/GL/en/Issues/Driving-growth/Middle-class-growth-in-emerging-markets.

EY. "Profit-or-lose. Balancing the growth-profit paradox for global consumer products companies and retailers in Asia's emerging markets," 2013; http://emergingmarkets.ey.com/profit-or-lose-2/.

EY's Rapid-Growth Markets Forecast, 2011; http://www.ey.com/Publication/vwLUAssets/Rapid_Growth_Markets_PDF/$FILE/Rapid-Growth-Markets.pdf.

EY. "Rethinking profitable growth: the productivity imperative for foreign multinationals in China," 2012; http://www.ey.com/Publication/vwLUAssets/Rethinking_profitable_growth_en/$FILE/Productivity-Rethinking-profitable-growth_en.pdf.

Farris, P., Moore, M. J., & Buzzell, R. *The Profit Impact of Marketing Strategy Project: Retrospect and Prospects* (Cambridge: Cambridge University Press, 2004).

"Fixing the future; building local jobs, income, and sustainability," PBS Documentary, 2012; http://fixingthefuture.org/.

Fujita, M. & Thisse, J. F. *Economics of Agglomeration, Industrial Location, and Regional Growth* (New York: Cambridge University Press, 2002).

Ghemawat, P. "Developing global leaders." *McKinsey Quarterly*, June 2012; http://www.google.com/url?sa=t&rct=j&q=&esrc=s&source=web&cd=1&ved=0CCsQFjAA&url=http%3A%2F%2Fwww.mckinsey.com%2Finsights%2Fleading_in_the_21st_century%2Fdeveloping_global_leaders&ei=CLk0U53jOMm4yQHL7IDABA&usg=AFQjCNE1cxIlvfg1Y6H-pFJ1z83Uaxgfhw&sig2=m8pfqmBxYRTOvJvLdzkBGw&bvm=bv.63808443,d.aWc.

Grove, A. *Only the Paranoid Survive: How to Exploit the Crisis Point That Challenges Every Company* (New York: Random Books, 1999).

Khanna, T. & Palepu, K. *Winning in Emergent Markets: A Roadmap for Strategy and Execution* (Boston, MA: Harvard Business School Publishing, 2010).

Knickerbocker, F. T. "Oligopolistic reaction and multinational enterprise." *International Executive*, 1973. 15(2):7–9.

Kotler, P., Ang, S. H., Leong, S. M., & Tan, C. T. *Marketing Management: An Asian Perspective* (Singapore: Prentice Hall, 1996).

Letelier, M. F., Flores, F., & Spinosa, C. "Developing productive consumers in emerging markets." *California Management Review*, 45(4):77–103. Product No. CMR263, 2003.

Meyer, K. E. & Tran, Y. T. "Market penetration and acquisition strategies for emerging markets." *Long Range Planning*, 2006. 39(2):177–197.

Monitoring Services. "Over 50% of global companies fail to make emerging markets information readily available for staff"; http://www.globalintelligence.com/insights-analysis/bulletins/over-50-of-global-companies-fail-to-make-emerging-#ixzz2Rb8pQnrg.

Moore, Geoffrey A. *Crossing the Chasm* (New York: HarperCollins, 2002).

Ohmae, K. *The Mind of the Strategist: The Art of Japanese Business* (New York: McGraw Hill, 1982).

O'Neil, J. *The Growth Map: Economic Opportunity in the BRICs and Beyond* (New York: Portfolio/Penguin, 2011).

Osburg, J. *Anxious Wealth: Money and Morality among China's New Rich* (Stanford: Stanford University Press, 2013)

Park, S. H., Zhou, N., & Ungson, G. R. *Rough Diamonds: The Four Successful Traits of Breakout Firms in BRIC* (San Francisco, CA: Jossey Bass, 2013).

Phelps, N. A. "External economies, agglomeration and flexible accumulation." *Transactions of the Institute of British Geographers, New Series*, 1992. 17(1):35–46. Published by the Royal Geographical Society (with the Institute of British Geographers): http://www.jstor.org/stable/622635.

Porter, M. E. *Competitive Strategy* (New York: Free Press, 1980).

Porter, M. E. *Competitive Advantage: Creating and Sustaining Superior Performance* (New York: Free Press, 1985).

Porter, M. E. "What is strategy?" *Harvard Business Review*, November–December 1996:1–20; http://weaddvalue2.web12.hubspot.com/Portals/188908/docs/hbr.what%20is%20strategy.pdf.

Pricewaterhouse Coopers. "Profitable growth strategies for the global emerging middle: learning from the 'next 4 billion' markets." 2012. http://www.pwc.in/en_IN/in/assets/pdfs/publications-2012/profitable-growth-strategies.pdf.

"Profit-or-Lose: balancing the growth-profit paradox for global consumer products companies and retailers in Asia's emerging markets." EYG no. EN0519. CSG/GSC2013/1164313; ED 1015(2013):12–15.

Quelch, J. & Jocz, K. *All Business Is Local: Why Place Matters More Than Ever in a Global, Virtual World* (New York: Portfolio/Penguin, 2012).

Reich, R. *Aftershock: The Next Economy and America's Future* (New York: Vintage Books, 2010, 2011).

Ries, A. & Trout, J. *Positioning: A Battle for Your Mind* (New York: McGraw Hill, 2001).

Rogers, Everett. *Diffusion of Innovation* (3d ed.) (New York: Free Press, 1963).

Scalability. Wikipedia, http://en.wikipedia.org/wiki/Scalability.

Shankar, S., Ormiston, C., Bloch, N., Schaus, R., & Vishwanath, V. "How to win in emerging markets," *MIT Sloan Management Review*, 49(3):18–24. Product No. 49309, 2008.

Sharma, R. *Breakout Nations: In Pursuit of the Next Economic Miracles* (New York: W. W. Norton, 2012).

Spence, M. *The Next Convergence: The Future of Economic Growth in a Multispeed World* (New York: Farrar, Straus and Giroux, 2011).

Sternberg, R. & Wennekers, S. "Causes and effects of new business creation: empirical evidence from the Global Entrepreneurship Monitor (GEM)." *Small Business Economics*, 2005. 24(3):323–334.

Stiglitz, J. *The Price of Inequality: How Today's Divided Society Endangers Our Future* (New York: W. W. Norton, 2012, 2013).

The Rise of China's Middle Class. Wikiinvest; http://www.wikinvest.com/concept/Rise_of_China's_Middle_Class.

Weisstein, E. W. "Inflection Point." From *MathWorld*—A Wolfram Web; http://mathworld.wolfram.com/InflectionPoint.html.

Wheelan, T. L. & Unger, D. J. *Strategic Management and Business Policy* (Upper Saddle River, NJ: Prentice Hall, 2006).

Wilson, D. "Dreaming with BRICs: The Path to 2050" Goldman Sachs, 2003; http://www.goldmansachs.com/our-thinking/archive/brics-dream.html.

Wilson, W. & Ushakov, N. "Brave New World Categorizing the Emerging Market Economies—A New Methodology," SKOLKOVO Emerging Market Index (February 2011).

Zhang, L. In Search of Paradise: Middle-Class Living in a Chinese Metropolis (New York: Cornell University Press, 2010).

About the Authors

Andrew Cosgrove is a consumer products expert with extensive emerging markets experience. Currently, he is the Global Lead Analyst for Consumer Products and Retail at EY, responsible for conducting research and driving EY's perspective on the sector, identifying emerging company strategies and business models, and pinpointing key implications for clients. Previously, Andrew had roles at McKinsey & Company and Mars, Incorporated, including five years in Asia identifying new business opportunities and entry strategies. His perspectives on the market are frequently quoted in publications including the *Financial Times*, the *Wall Street Journal*, and Just-Food.com. He can be reached at acosgrove@uk.ey.com.

Seung Ho Park is Parkland Chair Professor of Strategy at China Europe International Business School. He was the Founding President of Samsung Economic Research Institute in China. He was the Executive Director at Skolkovo-EY Institute for Emerging Market Studies (IEMS) and Chair Professor of Strategy at Moscow School of Management SKOLKOVO. He is a leading expert on emerging market strategies with publications in most leading academic journals and frequent contributions to popular media, including the *Financial Times* and *Forbes*. He coauthored an award-winning book, *Rough Diamonds: The Four Successful Traits of Breakout Firms in BRIC Countries* (San Francisco, CA: Jossey Bass, 2013). He can be reached at spark@ceibs.edu.

Gerardo R. Ungson is the Y. F. Chang Endowed Chair Professor of International Business at the College of Business, San Francisco State University. He was formerly Senior Research Fellow at Skolkovo-EY Institute for Emerging Market Studies (IEMS). He coauthored an award-winning book, *Rough Diamonds: The Four Successful Traits of Breakout Firms in BRIC Countries* (San Francisco, CA: Jossey Bass, 2013). In addition to his work on emerging markets, he is currently engaged in poverty alleviation research in the Philippines. He can be reached at bungson@sfsu.edu.

Index

affordable innovation, 70–71, *See* exploration of relevant drivers
  brand loyalty, 70
  dynamics, 70
  impact of local firms, 71
  local markets, 70
agglomeration. *See* contiguous interconnectedness
  multiple variants, 37
Ajinomoto, 99
Avery, Jill, 34

Batra, Rajeev, 46
Best Buy, 15
Bottom-of-the-pyramid, 15
BRIC-Brazil, Russia, India and China, 3

Cadbury India Ltd, 41, 64
  competition with Nestle, 76
  use of visi-coolers, 68
Chattopadhyay, Amitava, 46
Ching Luh Group, 79
Chris Anderson. *See The Long Tail (Anderson)*
coalignment, 105–106, *See* PEC Framework
  autonomy to local management, 93
  centralization and decentralization, 92
  corporate culture and governance, 98
  differences between higher and lower performance, 92
  inadequate governance, 98
  inadequate supply chain, 98
  infrastructure as a problem, 96
  internal barriers to execution, 97
  leadership, organizational structure, and incentive system, 48
  locus of decision making, 92
  logic of contingency, 48
  market fragmentation, 96
  obstacles to execution, 94
  regulation as protectionism, 96
  supportive corporate cultures, 102
  unsupportive local culture, 98
Colgate Palmolive, 7
  development of in-house local talent, 103
  product innovation, 69
Competitive Strategy (Porter). *See* generic strategies, *See* Porter, Michael
  competitive scope of operations, 74
  distinction between strategy and advantage, 68
conspicuous consumption, 27

160

Index

contiguous interconnectedness, 5, 37–39, 39, *See* spatial concentration
aggregation, 35
clustering, 37
interlinked nodes, 38
learning, 38
locality, 38
network effects, 38
network theory and computer architecture, 39
spatial modality, 38
spillovers, 38
contradictions in emerging markets, 58

Decorvet, Roland, 79
differentiated product brands, 41
multi-branding, 109
relation to price points, 122

Economist Intelligence Unit. *See* Phase II Empirical Study
Emerging Market Studies (IEMS), 4
emerging markets, 3, 21
changing norms and preferences, 23
consumer goods and retailing, 146
consumption preferences, 23
even growth versus granularity, 109
growth rates, 109
middle class in China, 121
middle class in emerging markets, 24
middle class sectors, 109
Ernst & Young (EY), 5
exploring relevant drivers, 87–88, *See* PEC Framework
brand strength, 69
channel-management, 73
cost reduction and performance, 79
distribution, 69
high and low performing firms, 73
outsourcing and lean manufacturing, 79
price point, product quality, and product innovation, 68
sources of synergies, 71
value proposition, 47

FNBM (Malaysia), 81

globalization, 83–84, *See* localization
risks in application, 76
Google, 84
competition in China, 84
granular growth, 3, 109–110
application to uneven economic development, 54
"multi-speed" products, 56
relation to affordable innovation, 71
relation to dual-speed markets, 58
Tier, 1, 2, 3 and 4 markets, 35
Grove, Andrew, 26

Herbalife, 81
competition in China, 95
Hindustan Unilever India, 23
management development and reliable information, 103
products in detergent business, 75
use of dedicated human resource managers, 103

inflection points, 26–27, *See* multi-touch, engaged consumer
changes in consumer goods and retail environment, 53

Janelle, Paul, 58
Jocz, Katherine, 84
Johnson & Johnson (J &J), 73
JT International Berhad (Malaysia), 63

Kangshifu, 23
competition with Uni-President Products, 72
Kelti China, 64
Key Performance Indicators
market share growth, 53
operating profits, 53
Khanna, Tarun, 15, *See* institutional voids
institutional voids, 15
Kraft Malaysia, 40
management systems, 104

Lian Jiang Ching Luh Shoes, Ltd, 79
Limitations of the Study, 112
localization, 7, 100–101, 99–101, *See*
  coalignment
  applied to Cadbury-India, 101
  applied to FNBM (Malaysia), 81
  applied to Unilever Holdings
    (Malaysia), 100
  applied to Want Want China, 72
  as a learning process, 123
  ethnocentric blinders, 124
  investment in local talent, 99
  local investment as an imperative, 83
  local refinements of the global
    product, 23
  management of local teams, 100
  process, 7
  relation to affordable innovation, 70
  relation to decentralization, 92
  risk of overlocalization, 93
  risks, 58
Long Tail (Anderson), 4, 31, *See*
  non-normal distribution, *See*
  Pareto Distribution
  peripheral versus traditional
    mass-sales, 4
Low cost strategy, 3

market niche, 35
  competency-based learning, 35
  relational capital, 35
Marshall, Alfred, 37
Mass consumption markets, 4
Maxwell House, 24
McKinsey Study, 3
Mondolez China, 80
multinational corporations, 8
  inability to scale, 16
multinational firms
  differences between developed and
    emerging markets, 54

Nestle India, 41
  open decision making, 103
  use of multi-tiered branding, 77
Ng, Swee Leng, 80

Nike, 7
Norton, Michael, 34
Nthunzi, Godfrey, 55

Oaf, Ehab Abou, 16, 113–119
Ohmae, Kenichi, 31
Oreo, 24

Palepu, Krishnan, 15
PEC Framework, 5, 46, 48, 111–112
  external environment, 52
  summary of performance-
    differences, 111
  use as a roadmap, 125
Pellegrino, Yves, 58
Pepsi Co, 103
performance-based culture, 101–105
Phase II Empirical Study, 48–49
  case studies, 49
  cross-sectional data analysis, 49
  cross-sectional survey, 5
  differences in performance, 49
  disaggregated sample, 49
  high versus low performance, 50
  study of BRICs, 11
PIMS, 13–14
Porter, Michael, 14
positioning. *See* PEC Framework
  capital and equity markets, 54
  cultural differences, 122
  data analytics, 59
  demand volatility, 56
  differences in profitability, 62
  differences in short-term versus
    long-term thinking, 53
  differentiation defined, 52
  differentiation positioning, 46
  differentiation using power brands, 75
  expansion modes, 62
  focus on product categories, 121
  focus on profitability, 54
  importance of emerging markets, 61
  investments, 60
  Key Performance Indicators, 53
  perceptions of market share, 57
  performance indicators, 53

positioning—*Continued*
   positioning cost advantage, 46
   sources of funding, 61
   traditional versus emerging mindsets, 110
   unqualified growth, 53
   value proposition, 52
Procter & Gamble, 7
   competition with Johnson & Johnson, 73
   Whisper brand, 80
production-centric logic, 21
   relation to cost-based model, 22
profitable growth, 3
   applied to consumer goods and services, 8
   diversity in distribution, 64
   growth by acquisitions and diversification, 47
   management systems, 47
   positioning over time, 52
   process learning, 7
   sources of advantage, 68
   surging market niches, 4
profit-oriented culture. *See* coalignment
PT Cahaya Kalbar TBK, 86
PT Multi Bintang Indonesia, 86

Quelch, John, 84

Reich, Robert, 24
Rough Diamonds (Park et al), 6
   conditions for profitable growth, 11
   Successful Trait (Park et al), 5

Sampoerma. *See* Janelle, Paul
Sanone. *See* Pellegrino, Yves
scaling, 3, 14–15, 36
   differences in high and low performing firms, 74
   diseconomies of scale, 16
   scaling across, 37
   scaling in, 37
   traditional models, 3
   types of scaling, 36

Scaling the Tail..., 4, *See* Anderson, Chris
   aggregating high end brands, 35
   application to scaling, 40
   difference between scaling the tail and the long tail, 35
   differences between marketing and manufacturing, 122
   differences with mass sales, 7
   intangible mental linkages between market brands, 7
   locality in scaling, 38
   multi-brands and flanking, 7
   multibranding and flanking, 27
   normal distribution, 31
   requirements, 41
   shift from mass consumption to specialized niches, 32
   specialized market niches, 5
   traditional concept of value creation, 31
Sharma, Ruchir, 46
Smart Technologies, 24
Steer, David, 59
Stiglitz, Joseph, 24
Straddling the curve, 31
sustainable competitive advantage, 11
SWOT Analysis, 55

Tsai, Anthony, 15, 14–16

Ungson, Gerardo R, 13
Unilever, 7
   Shaki system, 104

Want Want China Holdings Limited, 41, 72–73
   focus on product innovation, 85
Waszyk, Helio, 79
Weber, Max, 37
Wilson, William T, 25

Yamaha (Thailand) Company, Ltd, 104

Zhang, Li, 27
Zhou, Nan, 13

Printed by Printforce, United Kingdom